FRANCES CAMPBELL-PRESTON was born in 1918, and is a younger daughter of the banker, Arthur Grenfell and his wife, Hilda Lyttelton. She was educated at St Paul's School. In 1938 she married Patrick Campbell-Preston, a young officer in the Black Watch. Following the Fall of France in 1940, Patrick was captured and eventually imprisoned in Colditz Castle. Frances served as an 'immobile' Wren in Scotland from 1941 to 1943.

After the war, they raised their young family, Patrick briefly commanding his regiment before ill-health brought his military career to an end. Following Patrick's death in 1960, Frances was appointed a lady-in-waiting to the Queen Mother, serving from 1965 until the Queen Mother's death in 2002. She was created a DCVO in 1990. She was a member of Argyll County Council from 1960 to 1964 and Chairman of the Children's Panel, Argyll and Bute, from 1970 to 1980. Dame Frances now lives in London and Scotland and is a great-grandmother. Her autobiography, *The Rich Spoils of Time*, was published in 2006.

GRANDMOTHER'S STEPS

Frances Campbell-Preston

THE DOVECOTE PRESS

First published in 2010 by The Dovecote Press Ltd
Stanbridge, Wimborne Minster, Dorset BH21 4JD

ISBN 978-1-904-34985-3

Designed by The Dovecote Press
Printed and bound in Spain by GraphyCems, Navarra

All papers used by The Dovecote Press are natural,
recyclable products made from wood grown in sustainable,
well-managed forests

A CIP catalogue record for this book is available
from the British Library

1 3 5 7 9 8 6 4 2

CONTENTS

ACKNOWLEDGEMENTS

Even this slim volume owes thanks to so many people. For the help with research into my forbears I owe considerable thanks to Mrs Krasinska, a descendant of Admiral Parker, my great-grandfather's brother-in-law and colleague, and to Mr Rob Well, a naval historian with great knowledge of Uruguay, and also to my cousin, Francis Grenfell, who is an expert in family history. Mark Hichens alerted me to the book by Alice Buchan, *A Scrap Screen*, and also provided me with *The Times* obituary to our mutual great-grandmother, Jane Lawley.

Nigel Jaques was generous in giving me quotes, as was Lady Charteris, allowing me to quote from her husband's address at Martin Gilliat's Memorial Service. The photograph of me on the first page is by Anya Campbell, to whom I am grateful.

As usual enormous thanks are due for the support and encouragement from family and friends, especially to Hugo Vickers whose enthusiasm and help for the project never failed to keep me afloat and to my son-in-law Alastair Campbell who helped edit and kept me on line regarding facts and dates.

EIGHTIES AND NINETIES

It was Queen Elizabeth the Queen Mother who first alerted me to the possibility that I might be on the threshold of my best decade yet. I had been her lady-in-waiting for thirty-five years, so I suggested that when I had reached the august age of 80, it was time to retire.

'Congratulations,' she said. 'You'll feel marvellous after you are 80.' How right she was!

I had not thought much about how I might feel at 80. Thus far it had seemed that when you reach certain watersheds such as 50 or 70, you felt much the same and you just carried on. I hadn't imagined I might be entering a Golden Age. If I had thought about it at all, I had imagined I would be set on the path to senility and uselessness.

I was aware that I was a member of a generation that stood to benefit from the rapid, in fact staggering advances made by medical science. We could go on living with new hips, hearts, knees and eyes, not to mention a large choice of life giving pills.

But I was conscious that, wonderful as these developments were, in many cases they merely prolonged life without many safeguards as to the quality of that life, and the downside meant prolonged suffering for many people.

I had had considerable exposure to this when writing letters on the Queen Mother's behalf. Many of those who wrote to her were elderly. Some were locked into lonely housing situations, often frightened and threatened by yobbish neighbours. Others had found friends and security in an old people's home, only to be told by some arbitrary authority that their home was to be closed and their way of life upended. And, of course, for many, great physical hardships eclipsed any joy. But lots of people do live to enjoy relatively good health, given a gene of longevity in the family and some good luck - and I am one of them.

We octogenarians (or should I say nonagenarians?) were born before television, penicillin, polio shots, frozen foods, plastic and the Pill. We got married and then lived together, (how quaint can you be?). We thought "fast food" was what you ate in Lent, and a "Big Mac" was an oversized raincoat. We had never heard of tape decks, Ipods, or even yoghurts. For us the term 'making out' referred to how you had done in your exams, a stud was something that fastened a collar to a shirt, and 'going all the way' meant staying on a double decker bus until you reached the bus depot. In our day, smoking was fashionable, grass was mown, a joint was a piece of meat and 'pot' was something you cooked it in.

So we have come a long way. What's it like ninety years on? Initially you don't wake up on your birthday feeling any different from the day before. Gradually you recognise that other people's perception of you has changed. They are apt to be surprised that you are still alive, they find it impressive that you can talk quite sensibly, and amazing that you can still walk. It begins to dawn on you that being 80 is more fun than being 60 or 70. At those ages, if you complain, others think you are just disgruntled. But at 80 you can flaunt your hearing aids, as well as discuss their digital miracles (and impress others that you know the word digital). Whereas once your children thought you were behind the times, they now boast of your dazzling prowess, and are entertained that you think Elton John is a horse that has won the Derby.

There are other advantages. You can be extravagant, explaining that if you don't spend it, the money will only go in death duties, and you can refuse to stay anywhere that has not got an en-suite bathroom. But best of all, clothes don't matter. You can even wear comfortable low-heeled shoes (the wrong colour) to a cocktail party – and cocktail parties are refreshingly rare in themselves because, for the first time in your life, you can admit that you loathe them and leave at once.

You are also no longer scared of making a fool of yourself. Early on in my eighties I broke my ankle, just as I was rather smugly thinking to myself how fit I was. I slipped on a patch of mud and all of a sudden came face to face with the fact that in my eighties I was sitting on a mud pat in a wood, unable to move, dependent on the hope that at some moment during the evening my family would realize I was missing and come and find me. Happily a visiting tourist, out for a walk, found me. I was lucky they beat the family to it.

Memories can be a source of pleasure. With luck, and possibly a bit of ingenuity and good management, bad ones can be mitigated or forgotten. While war time memories are not wholly pleasant, they remain a potent part of our psyche, but it is possible to reflect that, as a generation, if we 'had not stood alone' it could have all been much worse. Recently I confessed to a taxi driver that I felt a little guilty taking advantage of a subsidized taxi (as the old get in London). He patted me on the arm and said 'Don't you worry, love. You lot earned it.'

It can be fun to remember life as it was, but the dismal oldie who bemoans the past the whole time is in for a frustrating time. Often it is the past generation who have sown the seeds that make these later developments inevitable. Beating the drum of 'the good old days' should be muted. Just as often as the old resent children (who, it must be admitted make more noise at times than one can reasonably bear), old people can annoy the young, as this letter in *The Times* pointed out:

> Sir, As a child I regarded elderly people upholders of the standards of common courtesy and behaviour to others. Now in our thirties my wife and I increasingly observe that senior citizens are displaying bad manners. They often fail to acknowledge a door held open for them, or the offer of a seat on a train; we are regularly jostled in queues by oldies that appear unwilling to wait their turn. Have I

become intolerant or is the present generation of senior citizens less polite?

I well remember the days when I might have felt the same way, when the doings of the afternoon relentlessly took over, fetching the children from school, and never finding the time to be punctual or to fit everything in. I used to long for an afternoon when you could just sit with a book and possibly go to sleep in a chair. Now that I can, I do it with a vengeance. It's a rich feeling.

It must be admitted that there is one necessary ingredient to make it almost easy to enjoy one's old age, and that is to have the support of a family of all ages. And although friends die and are all missed, young friends come to take their places. Although it is never quite the same, they do have the merit of changing your angle or perception and keeping your mind on the present and even the future.

In the end, we are old. There is no evading it. For me, Dame Mary Warnock surmises the feeling perfectly:

> I love self-indulgently reading diaries I kept in 1940, a world infinitely remote. I know there are things that I shall never do and things I shall never see again. Or live in an exquisite Queen Anne house, or even do the things I truly loved, such as having babies and playing in an orchestra . . . or sex. That I understand them without inappropriate hankering.
>
> And I am hugely grateful not to have to bother whether what I eat or drink is healthy or if I am the right weight.

She goes on to describe this time of life as a second

adolescence. She says that 'adolescence was a time, of poetry music and Wordsworthian sentiments about nature.' I drink to that.

All these things, and far more, seem so much fresher once you settle for old age and have the time and solitude to enjoy them.

I was asked the other day what my plans for the future were. It was hard not to giggle. Obviously death is my future, but people seem to think that if you do not mention it, it will go away. It is not death, though - it is the anteroom to death. I do fear being sustained in a zombie like state, well past my death date.

But 'amidst life is death' and that is as it has always been. Of my own family of seven siblings only I survive. So it is not a new idea. But for us, perhaps death is an easy concept to grasp, nurtured and sustained all our lives by our Christian Faith which led us to the belief, and the hope of reunion. I trust my funeral will be cheerful and that the coffin will be carried out to the tune of the *Regimental March of the Black Watch*, to alert my husband that I am on my way.

That is my plan for the future and it makes me smile.

THE CORSAIR AND THE PRESIDENT

Nowadays great-grandparents are two a penny. I have a great-grandson who is 20, so we live in the same world. Naturally, as a child, I took no interest in the history of great-grandparents but once I found myself elevated to that role, I felt an urge to find out who my predecessors were.

My great-grandparents were born at the end of the 18th century or at the beginning of the 19th century, nearly 200 years ago. I can only know them from documents and in letters which give an indication of their characters, and of the way they lived.

Admiral John Grenfell of the Brazilian Navy was Lord Cochrane's second-in-command and 'performed many famous exploits, notably the cutting out and destruction of the Spanish flagship *Esmeralda* in the midst of an armed squadron.' He was one of my great-grandfathers.

John Pascoe Grenfell was born in Battersea in 1800. When he was 18 he joined the Marine division of the East India Company. Shortly after this he left for Brazil to join Admiral

Lord Cochrane, a British Admiral who, after a chequered career in the Royal Navy, sailed away with William Parker, another British Naval officer, to join the Brazilian Navy as its Commander, and to fight in South America with the intention of freeing the States from the Spanish and Portuguese. Unless you are a genius as an historian, it is impossible to unravel the history of South America at that time. Whichever way it was, his was an adventurous life.

John Pascoe inspired many stories. In one skirmish, he discovered that the Captain on the opposing side was an Irishman, so he invited him, through his megaphone, to join battle – but to come and have tea with him afterwards. The reply was a salvo which took off my great-grandfather's arm.

This is where my great-grandmother made her first appearance. Her parents, my great-great-grandparents were called Antonio and Maria Corbella Masini. The Masinis were originally an Italian family and came from the district of Livano in Tuscany. They were considerable ship owners and had a large art collection. They also owned olive groves. As Napoleon advanced over Europe, they became anxious about their position and decided to move, with South America their eventual goal.

Before leaving for South America, they paused in Cadiz where my great-great-grandmother, Maria Corbella, met my great-great-grandfather. Her father was the King of Spain's doctor/surgeon. Her mother was a Maid of Honour to the Queen and they seem to have been well connected to the Spanish

Royal Court. Eventually the Masinis decided to continue their journey to Uruguay and and settled in Montevideo. Great-great-grandfather Antonio Masini married Maria Corbella in the Cathedral at Montevideo.

Before they left Spain, Antonio made a good deal with the King of Spain, the King appointing him his official Corsair in South America. A 'Corsair' is really a pirate with a slightly disguised name. He was encouraged to use his considerable fleet to sink British merchantmen and take a share of the prize money. This was a most profitable business and he rapidly became extremely prosperous. It is said that Antonio Masini had 122 slaves, ran an enormous garden which provided most of the vegetables for the district, that he also had a meat factory and a large house in the town, not to mention an unspecified acreage and ranch in the Argentine.

But, towards the end of his life, his affairs were the subject of an investigation and he was involved in prolonged litigation. He became ill in the last two years of his life, subsided into a coma and died at the age of 47.

His widow Maria was left to cope with his complicated legacy. His estates and properties were confiscated or fell into a 'testamentary process' whence they disappeared without trace. He owned big olive groves, which did not even appear in the inheritance, as well as the ships of which the family were stripped without explanation. The frigate *Isabella*, loaded with ingots of gold and silver and a quantity of jewels, was kept in Brazil, but nothing could ever be salvaged from it, in spite of Maria Corbella travelling to Brazil accompanied by her children to obtain their release.

So this was the family into which my great-grandmother, Maria Dolores Masini, was born and to which John Pascoe came to be nursed after he lost his arm. His misfortune no doubt started the romance which ended in their marriage. It is strange that less than a decade after the Corsair's death, John Pascoe and his friend William Parker, both British citizens, each married a Masini daughter. I wonder what they felt about their late father-in-law sinking British ships!

After their marriage Maria continued to live in Montevideo while John Pascoe pursued his career as a naval officer in various South American navies, being engaged in naval battles in the River Platte and elsewhere. In the end he became disillusioned by the political scene. On one occasion he wrote a letter to his brother-in-law, Romano, who had become a senior member of the ruling government of Uruguay.

This letter was written from his ship in La Bahia. He explained that his ship was stranded there:

> The President does not want me to leave until another ship takes over from me. But I have asked the Minister so forcefully that they must pay attention. We have just a month of provisions left.

He went on to describe the uprising by what he called 'the Negroes', that he was presumably engaged in suppressing, and said how gallant they were in the face of overwhelming odds. He seemed to admire the rebels and questioned the side which he was meant to be upholding:

It is right that those involved in such an offence should be punished with death if we consider the rights of the white people, but what do you say about the civilisation of the Bahia Judges who used torture on these unhappy creatures? Ramon, the greatest blight on America is African slavery. It is a public crime, an offence so atrocious against the human race that in this century of justice all those who permit or defend such barbarism will not escape the deserved punishment that a just God is preparing for them! The magnanimous act of the British government, an action without equal in the history of the world, giving liberty to all Negroes in all its colonies and paying their value to their owners is the first act of a drama beginning in the Theatre of the World. It no doubt contains tragic scenes but it will end with total freedom of this unfortunate race.

Use your strength and influence to free our homeland of the evils with which a corrupt administration and some vile Portuguese have loaded it, cry out against the miserable short-sighted policy of populating this beautiful country with ignorant Negroes.

I want to withdraw myself as soon as possible from a struggle, which does not concern me and which could be terrible. I have served the common cause of America as much in Peru as in Brazil, in all the wars of their independence. The Pacific and the Atlantic have had my blood, I lost my right arm in a war of oppression and I do not want to lose my life in another.

Clearly he felt passionately about his causes. Was he ahead of his time? – also perspicacious perhaps?

It is rather odd that, in spite of the fact that William Parker and John Pascoe were both British citizens, they chose to communicate with each other in Spanish, the dominant language in their families. Many of John Pascoe's logs, which still exist, are written in Spanish. He always kept his British citizenship and apparently had Queen Victoria's express permission to serve abroad!

While John Pascoe pursued his career as a naval officer, Maria had her hands full bringing up children as they produced a family of nine children, of which one of their daughters, Sophia, was my grandmother.

In 1846 John Pascoe returned to Liverpool with his family, where he became the Brazilian Consul with the rank of Rear Admiral. The Brazilian Navy had commissioned a considerable shipping programme which John Pascoe was to be responsible for over seeing. From then on, the whole family was brought up in England and very rarely returned to Uruguay. John Patrick seems to have concentrated on getting them subsumed into his Grenfell family. But he was recalled to fight in one more rebellion in South America.

Photographs of John Pascoe reveal a charming, handsome young man, dressed in uniform with an open and smiling face. He is what my granddaughters would probably call 'dishy.' Later on as a small old man with one arm and with a long white beard, he looks rather endearing. Maria appears in her photographs as a good-looking lady with an engaging smile.

In the early 19th century my great-great-grandparents on my maternal side were quite different. While Antonio Mansini was happily sinking British ships in the Atlantic, another pair of great-great-grandparents came from Yorkshire and lived both there and in Curzon Street in London. He was the 1st

Lord Wharncliffe. He was a member of Peel's Cabinet which came into power after the defeat of Melbourne. He became Lord President of the Council in 1841.

On one occasion he wrote to his wife describing a visit he made to Windsor Castle, a date he much looked forward to. They lunched first, and after the Council meeting were told to amuse themselves as they liked till five o'clock, in which interval several of them walked to Eton to see their sons or grandsons. 'To walk to Eton and back across the field after a Council meeting, to ride out in Windsor Park with the tireless little Queen, to dine and play whist with the Prince Consort after dinner, and then stay up listening to Wellington's campaigning anecdotes till after midnight made up a strenuous day.' I wonder if the Council discussed how to deal with Corsairs.

He had a large family and his third son was my great-grandfather, James Stuart-Wortley, always referred to as Jem. He was 'naturally filled with gaiety and optimism.' He was musical and loved the theatre, but was ready to carry on with the family tradition in politics in spite of his father writing to him when he was planning to become an MP:

Bad and precarious as the trade of a politician has always been it has now become 10 hundred times worse than ever and holds out to a younger brother nothing but poverty and disappointment.

In spite of this, Jem went into politics after having qualified as a lawyer, a career in which he looked like being progressively successful.

He married Jane Lawley, the only daughter of Lord Wenlock

after a lengthy courtship during which she turned him down for a number of years. Jane was described as having a quiet manner which concealed shyness, a resolute will, inflexible standards of behaviour and great personal courage. She passed on her looks, her height and short-sighted blue eyes to her descendants.

The first ten years of their lives were happy and successful. He became Solicitor-General and they lived in Carlton Gardens near the House of Commons where they were much 'resorted to as an hospitable centre by friends such as Mr Gladstone, Mr Sidney Herbert and other distinguished members of Parliament.' On one occasion they hosted an historic dinner party where one of the guests was Mr Gladstone aged 42. There was a critical debate going on in the House of Commons where Disraeli was making what was seen as being a formidable speech lasting three hours! Mr Gladstone was to make the return speech. The assembled dinner party tried to persuade him not to go and take part, as they felt that Mr Disraeli would wipe the floor with him. Gladstone refused to be daunted and went to the House of Commons and made a masterly speech as well which apparently lasted almost as long as Mr Disraeli's.

But this delightful state of affairs was soon to end. Jem had a bad riding accident and was crippled for the rest of his life. His legal career ceased and the financial position became constrained. They removed from Carlton Gardens to smaller establishments and, besides tending to her husband, Jane had to take on the running of the house and the family finances which was rare for a Victorian lady.

With a large family of two sons and five daughters, they eventually ended up living in St James's Place, a cul-de-sac which runs parallel to St James's Street. In spite of its geographical position it was not looked on as a smart location in those days. Jem lived on for over 20 years and once he had come to terms with the fact that he would not walk again, 'his disposition turned again to sunniness.' But the tone of family life seems to have been set entirely by my great-grandmother Jane.

In spite of living in Belgravia, she would leave her house in days when slumming had not as yet become fashionable, and go quite alone 'to penetrate the darkest and most forlorn recesses of Bedfordbury' and visit the sick whom she tended with her own hand and who looked on her as a ministering angel. She became one of the founders of the East London Nursing Association. She took a great interest in convalescent homes and asylums. She also became President of the United Women's Emigration Association, an organisation founded in the 1880s to assist the surplus women problem in the United Kingdom and to assist educated British women to emigrate by finding them employment usually as governesses or clerks, in Australia, New Zealand, South Africa and Canada. This could seem to us just as peculiar an activity as being a corsair. According to her obituary in *The Times* in 1900 'to capture some of the good deeds which she did would far exceed the limits that are at our command.'

When she was known to be dying, Mr Gladstone, a long time friend and admirer, wrote:

> I am certainly reminded by your letter of the struggle between life and death now going on. It is cheering to reflect that be the end what it may it must be good. She has fought a good fight has gone through great trials and has proved herself a noble Christian soul whose memory will be a treasure to all belonging to her.

She once had her photograph taken by Julia Margaret Cameron and it was called "Resignation" and was sold extensively; *The Times* reporting again 'and a more perfect Representative of that virtue could not be conceived.' She had a wonderful memory and laced her conversation with 'the rich spoils of time – They abounded with political and social anecdotes which to congenial listeners were full of instruction and entertainment.'

I wonder if she may have been a bore?

THE ROYAL HOSPITAL, CHELSEA

The Royal Hospital, Chelsea was an important place for our family in my childhood. Up to the age of thirteen it was a second home. We frequently stayed there and we often visited it.

My grandfather was the last Governor to be appointed there for life, and he lived on for the best part of 20 years. He was General Sir Neville Lyttelton. He was given this sinecure after long service in the regular army, during the course of which he had been in the Rifle Brigade and served in India and Canada. He had been a general in the Boer War and was the first ever Chief of the Imperial General Staff.

In his memoirs, he wrote: 'The tenure of the post was for life and in all respects it is the most desirable billet, a charming house, pleasant surroundings and certain pecuniary advantages. I have spent my active life among soldiers and now in my declining years I find myself associated with veterans, more or less of my own standing.'

There were some notable veterans, four surviving from the Crimean War. One of them told my grandfather that the reason he had enlisted for the Crimea was that two of his friends had a particular dislike of the Russians. He also remembered Florence Nightingale, that she gave him his first hot meal, and he added the remark she 'was a fine woman who had no thought of marriage.'

This enables me to say that as a child I shook the hands of four veterans of the Crimean War of 1854, in the 1920s.

My grandparents inhabited the whole house. The rooms now called the State Rooms were their reception rooms, simply called the drawing room, the small sitting room, and the dining room. It was the most beautiful house in London and besides the State Rooms it had many bedrooms. The kitchen was in the basement and the food came up in a lift that was operated by pulling a rope. But in the main part of the house was a lift which worked with the normal button, a rare luxury at that time.

Both my grandparents were members of large families – my grandfather having eight brothers and five sisters and my grandmother five sisters and two brothers. This meant that Chelsea was a home to many cousins. Although my grandparents had grandchildren of their own they still ran an open house for their extended family of nephews and nieces. Amongst the cousins frequently to be found there were Edward Ford who went on to be Assistant Private Secretary to George VI and The Queen for many years, and Elizabeth Alington who became a Prime Minister's wife when she married Lord Home – later Sir Alec Douglas-Home.

Amongst my grandmother's nieces was Susan Grosvenor

who married John Buchan. Another niece was due to have a baby in the First World War. Since she lived in Northern Ireland, it was thought more convenient for her to come to London. The Governor's house was vacated to make room for her to have the baby.

When I was small it never occurred to me that my grandparents did not own this delectable place. It was run on feudal lines like a village where everyone knew everyone else.

When we were in London, church on Sunday was always in the Chapel. Attendance by the old pensioners was compulsory so before every Sunday service there was a parade which my grandfather inspected in his uniform, complete with spurs and feathered hat. He was a tall straight-backed man with a large drooping grey moustache and he made quite a figure talking to the groups as he inspected them. During the service he would clank up the aisle in his spurs to read the lesson from the pulpit. These services left us with a pleasant legacy of knowing the 1662 matins service practically by heart for the rest of our lives.

There are many memories of life at the Royal Hospital. The flower shows in the summer, not nearly so large or as they are now, were always attended by the King and Queen. My grandfather came from a notoriously absent-minded family. On occasion King George V came to the show with Queen Mary. Neither the King nor my grandfather were particularly interested in the exhibits. So they wandered off to sit on a seat where they had an enjoyable conversation all afternoon. My grandfather afterwards remarked what a nice afternoon he had had talking to a charming man whose face he knew very well but could not for his life think who he was.

An abiding memory is of my grandmother's tea parties in the drawing room. A round tea table would be brought in and opened up. Then it was laid with a silver tray on which was put a kettle balanced on a silver stand with a container beneath it, inside which was a gas flame to keep the kettle boiling. There was a silver teapot and a silver tea caddy, which had a little scoop spoon which apparently dwelt amongst the tea leaves. There was the silver milk jug and sugar bowl, and up to a dozen teacups. The table was covered with delicious food – large cakes, small cakes, tomato and possibly cucumber sandwiches, Gentleman's Relish, scones, jam and butter and toast as well. It was a noble display and not at all unusual as this was the norm at that time.

Unfortunately private photography was in a very early stage and rarely used indoors and I always regret that there is no photograph in any archive of this scene. At these tea parties the guests were sometimes few in number, just some intimates, and at others a larger company. Besides invited guests, quite often passing friends would drop in. My grandmother had an eclectic circle of friends and anyone from the Archbishop of Canterbury, perhaps Andre Maurois, the French writer, Reginald Blount, a much respected Chelsea resident and historian, would arrive. Or my mother's ex-governess, almost certainly living on the remnants of an income, would appear and happily eat a rare good meal. Occasionally we would be allowed to join, in, in order to hand round the plates and see that everyone was fed.

The other memory is of my grandparents sitting in their cosy sitting room, my grandfather with a pewter mug won for some victory at school, on a shelf beside him, in which he kept his penny whistles. We would climb onto his knee and he would play us nursery rhyme tunes, his favourite being 'Pop goes the weasel.'

I cannot help thinking that it must have been incredibly cold, as the rooms in the Royal Hospital are large and high. There was no form of central heating, electrical fires not yet being usual. But I do remember blazing coal fires in every room including our night nursery, where we went to bed with the lovely shapes of flames flickering on the ceiling. What the administration must have entailed for all this makes one's modern mind boggle.

When we stayed with our grandparents we always had breakfast, followed by family prayers for the whole household, in the dining room, and we also lunched there, so no nursery meals were carried up by footmen. This meant one sat mostly as an observer taking in the conversation that went round the table and remembering for the rest of one's life people such as Sir Edward Grey, Mrs Asquith, known as Margot, Dorothy Ward, the daughter of Mrs Humphrey Ward, the children's novelist, who had employed my grandmother in her early married life. My grandfather, although absent-minded, also had a prodigious memory and seemed to be able to recite the whole of the *Pickwick Papers* by heart, and quite often obliged.

To have had the luck to start one's life with such happy memories in such a lovely place was indeed a privilege.

HILDA MARGARET GRENFELL

It is difficult to write objectively about one's mother. Hilda was an erratic person but lived an extremely difficult life. By nature she was imaginative and impractical, but she was forced to live a life entirely dominated by the practical. The maelstrom of my father's financial affairs meant that she was constantly dealing with problems both financial, which she never entirely understood, and logistical. We moved from big houses to little houses and back again.

She was a conscientious mother to seven children – three stepchildren and four daughters of her own. She was always there to take on our moods and experiences and traumas and even if she got solutions wrong it was certainly not from lack of trying.

The ground of her being was her religion and her faith. Her faith was immovable. This affected everything she did (although it is difficult to equate this with our house moves). It meant that often she was intellectually ahead of the times. She took our education and well-being much to heart. Her stepchildren were as devoted to her as were her own four daughters and

I think we would all claim to have had exceptionally happy childhoods in a close knit family.

One of the constant searches in her life was how to believe in science and combine it with her religion. If Hilda espoused a cause she went for it, all out, and nothing was allowed to stand in its way. So, when in her seventies, she found the writings of Teilhard de Chardin, the Jesuit priest, and his scientific books she felt she had reached her Holy Grail. After my father's death she was free to go wherever she wanted to. This included going to Paris and finding de Chardin's archive. There she discovered that although his big books were being translated by experts there were several un-published essays which she determined to translate and publish. They never were published in the end in spite of the fact she had persuaded Mrs Collins, the wife of William Collins, the publisher, to take them. Mr Collins met my brother Reggie and said gloomily: 'My wife and your mother are going to bankrupt me.'

Hilda did not hesitate to target friends and relations if she needed hospitable lodgings from which to pursue her cause. Therefore, when she found she needed to pick the brains of various knowledgeable specialists at Oxford, Lavinia Mynors, the daughter of her aunt Hester Alington, immediately came to mind. Lavinia's husband, Roger Mynors, was Professor of Latin at Oxford. An excerpt from Lavinia's diaries explained how life unfolded for them over a weekend:

March 1965

Late home. Roger had drowsed off, but stirred himself to impart the sobering news that Hilda Grenfell wanted a bed for tomorrow night, as Hermione can't have her till Sunday. (Can't have her in that great house?)

Saturday

Roger further imparted that Hilda was coming at once. Shot out to the shops and back, and in due course she turned up with a wild eyed taxi driver with whom she had visited every house in the neighbourhood including the Examination Schools looking for number 34 (Mynors lived at 14). She wants the Professor of Eastern Religions. We went through her attaché case looking for the facts, and I read every piece of paper she took out as fast as I could, hoping to get a line on what was going forward. In the end we chose All Souls and I left her there at her request, but retired to the window of the Bank opposite to keep observation.

Accordingly I ran into her when she retired defeated, but could not prevent her taking an hour's walk and trying again. After that she fell asleep so profoundly on the sofa that I thought she had left us, and on waking could not imagine who I was nor where she was, nor why, which I was in no position to tell her.

After more sleep I drove her to the Old Ladies Home, to visit the melancholy daughter of Archbishop Maclagan. This was a great success. I made a plan that Roger should drive her to Hermione's tomorrow morning, as she is one of the most tiring conversationalists I know. It isn't only Teilhard de Chardin, though he comes in every ten minutes, but it's the continental aspect of the thing which must be called something like Catholic Advance. Perpetual Abbés pop up – let alone the Jesuits who seem to be making a corner in Teilhard de Chardin, and all have written thoughtful and penetrating books. Roger and I say 'yes, yes they

33

<u>are</u> wonderful,' and feel madder and madder.

Roger helped her with Latin translations from de Chardin which was good. But she now says that she can't go till after lunch tomorrow as Hermione can't have her till her lunch party has gone.

The Professor of Eastern Religions is hiding – and very sensible too – Roger is making himself delightful, but I think will call a meeting of the Society for the Protection of those who marry Lytteltons – sub Branch Alingtons. I went to bed with two vegamins.

Sunday

All of us to the Cathedral. Abbés and Teilhard de Chardin and Preston-Campbells for breakfast topics. I never did meet anyone called Preston-Campbell, but I see it is her daughter. Our guest sat in her room all the morning translating de Chardin and I went to church. Lunch madder than ever, then Roger took her to Steeple Aston. She is quite beautiful, indomitable and perfectly impracticable.

Resumed the conduct of my shattered life by writing these memoirs – break them off as the telephone rings to say Hilda is coming back as Hermione can't put her up.

Roger returned and I broke it to him that his labour had been in vain. He was greatly interested. Steeple Aston had seemed to him in the last stages of dereliction and a tall grey-haired woman gardening had taken no notice of their arrival, so he had come away. Never mind, we thought, she's said she's all right for dinner – so we relaxed.

However, soon after six, Roger going out to leave some notes, found Hilda's luggage in the hall. At this point we became reconciled to the situation as something terrible must have happened – besides it roused our detective instincts and we set out to find her. We thought she was ashamed to come back and would wander from one hot-dog stall to another till she dropped. Anyway I found her at once in the Lodge of All Souls laying birds-lime for the Professor of Eastern Religions. She had meant 'to get a sandwich somewhere and go to Evensong' but I stopped all that and brought her back and gave her stimulants.

A very cheerful evening then took place, and I showed her photographs of Mrs A in youth and Aunt Syb's diaries and generally kept the conversation under control. What's more the Professor of Eastern Religions positively rang up and said he could see her tomorrow morning – so she went to bed blissful, clasping his latest book which I found for her in Blackwell's yesterday.

Monday
Roger leapt up early and went to Cambridge in the car. I had to go to work too, and I wasn't totally averse from letting Hilda see that there was some work to be done – still we had quite a leisurely breakfast, and Susie Tweedsmuir has been corralled to give her lunch at the Radcliffe and get her to her train. So I left her (sparing a thought to the Professor of Eastern religions – little he knows poor chap) and went off to tell . . . what we have been up to.

Roger back latish – 'Are we alone?' says he incredulously. We were.

When my brother Reggie got his copy of de Chardin, he remarked that he had difficulty in understanding them in English and he couldn't imagine how our mother had understood them in French. I met a professor of theology, who was one of the academics engaged in translating the full works and he told me that although my mother may have slipped up on the odd word, she had completely caught the spirit of the writer and possibly better than the official translators. It was rather an impressive last achievement for an octogenarian.

Soon after completing the translation of several of de Chardin's unpublished short essays, all of which were circulated round the family, my mother sadly retreated into illness which ended in her death.

THREE FRIENDS

SIR MARTIN GILLIAT

Friends are one of the most important features of life and
it is impossible to chronicle them all. But Martin was a
special friend, not only to me but to many others.

On his 75th birthday, Nigel Jaques, the Eton housemaster,
penned this poem for him:

Dear Martin, we greet you
At seventy-five
Your friends are thankful
That you are still alive

Each day before breakfast
Your duties begin
As letters and papers
Flow ceaselessly in

Each day at eleven
You dutifully stand
With programme and speeches
Prepared in your hand

Our blessed Queen Mother
(I make bold to say)
Relies on you wholly
To order her day
There's racing at Ascot
You've looked up the form
The Press are all clamouring
You weather the storm

There are people to dinner
You work at the seating
You dish out the grub
When the Beagles are meeting

In Scotland you tramp
In cloth cap over moors
In London you're robed
As a Doctor of Laws

Unfailingly thoughtful
To all, high or low,
You are properly honoured
As G.C.V.O.

When duties are over
It pleases you most
To entertain friends
As impeccable host

The warmth of your presence
Keeps boredom at bay
There is pleasure in plenty
At 31A

Your pour out the Gin
At a speed supersonic
The only complaint is
We can't taste the tonic!

A theatrical angel
You go to the play
The bookings are rising
You hope it will pay

But winning or losing
You're never defeated
And when you go racing
The bookies feel treated

Whatever awaits you
Of laughter or tears
Well done, dear Martin
For Seventy-five years.

Martin Gilliat came in to my life during the war when he became a prisoner of war with my husband Patrick. For Patrick he was an old friend, as although Martin was several years younger than Patrick they had overlapped at prep school, Eton, and then in the Army in India.

To keep information going during the war between families we, the next of kin, had started a round robin news-sheet to share news from the Prisoner of War camps and it fell to me to circulate it. This led to my meeting Martin's parents whenever I came to London. I would put my bike on the train to Welwyn and bicycle from the station. The Gilliats were an endearing couple and lifelong fishermen. It seemed their holidays were invariably spent fishing, mostly in Scotland. Foreign parts held no interest for them at all . . . Mrs Gilliat used to attend family get-togethers held by the 60th Rifles, Martin's Regiment, and give me pungent and forthright views of what she thought of everyone. I always enjoyed visiting them.

Martin Gilliat became the Queen Mother's Private secretary. He joined a few years after the King's death and served for nearly 40 years. He was a considerable lynch pin in the household, and a strong character, who helped her to rebuild her life after she became a widow. Martin was an obvious choice, having been trained in many overseas posts after the war. He had been a prisoner of war in Colditz, where, amongst his fellow prisoners, he made friends with John Elphinstone, who was the Queen Mother's nephew.

He was an imposing figure, tall, redheaded, with beetling eyebrows. He had had a wide experience both in India and Australia, and from those assignments he had come back with many friends and contacts. Martin was a loyal friend and kept in contact with his friends all over the world. He used all these assets in his service to the Queen Mother.

He also had a wonderful sense of humour and a gift for breaking the ice and diffusing any awkward situation that might arise. On a foreign tour, conversation could become strained at a banquet which often lasted several hours. When sitting next to ladies, Martin, although a bachelor, would get them to talk of their children, and when their conversation came to an end, he kept the talk going by inventing a family of his own. This rapidly became an hilarious story. He invented an extremely neurotic and hopeless wife who was unable to cope with their large family, all of whom were in trouble. Martin would then consult these ladies, saying they obviously had great experience, and could they advise him what he should do? This story grew as our travels went on.

He usually had one or two sons in prison, while the others were involved in various escapades. Martin confessing to having a guilty conscience because he was enjoying himself on tour with the Queen Mother rather than at home dealing with his family and their terrible misdemeanours. It became compulsive listening for all of us, and while we made other conversation, we were apt to be listening with one ear to the next instalment about Martin's mythological family. Even the Queen Mother was not beyond allowing her attention to wander to this saga.

Martin also had what we all thought some dangerous beliefs. One was that if you made a derogatory remark about someone, it was safer to be standing beside them as they would never think that the remark referred to them.

It was Martin who suggested me as a possible lady-in waiting. He was a marvellous colleague to work with as you were never quite sure what might happen next.

In Australia, we had just left by train, and the Queen Mother had settled into her compartment, when Martin bustled in announcing that we must now get the automatic arm. I was relatively new to the job and was surprised by this announcement. "The automatic arm?" I asked. "Well, yes," said Martin. "You wouldn't expect the Queen Mother to wave during this long journey and at every station we pass, so we have an automatic arm . . . " I confess I was taken in at first.

On another occasion, when we were in Canada and were flying from Toronto to Niagara Falls in a small, somewhat antiquated plane provided by the Canadian Air Force, a thick mist developed over Niagara and our pilot, who had no radar, found it difficult to land. So we flew round and round the landing ground for some hairy time until, finally, he was able to land. As we left the aircraft, Martin turned to the polite young aircraft man seeing us off and said: 'Amy Johnson would have loved this plane.' Mercifully the young airman beamed.

At his memorial service in St Martin's in the Fields which was attended by over 2,000 people of all ages, his lifelong friend, Lord Charteris, summed him up in a brilliant address which I quote:

St Martin in the Fields – 8 July 1993
'It is written that we are to praise no man before his death, but that in the end shall be the exposing of his works.'
I believe and hope that Martin would take it as a compliment that I should begin this address in his praise and honour with those words. They are the words with which John Blacman, Confessor to King Henry VI, Founder of Eton College, began his memorial to the murdered King.

Martin was a devoted son of Eton, he flourished there as a boy and remained faithful to the College all his life. Indeed, one of his last official engagements was to accompany Queen Elizabeth to Eton on Her Majesty's annual visit. Eton meant a great deal to him. He was, of course, vastly more competent and sensible than The Founder but was, like him, a man of benignity and faith.

It would NOT, however, have been easy for anyone who saw Martin in the last weeks of his life to obey John Blacman's injunction NOT to praise him!

He was run to a shadow, visibly dying, jaundiced as a yellow guinea, scarcely able to walk across Colour Court from his apartment to his office at Clarence House, where at his desk he found some ease in continuing with Queen Elizabeth's full understanding and blessing, to work for her as he had done for 37 years. In spite of pain, weakness and nausea he remained courageous, humourous and of wonderful morale until the end: it was NOT possible not to praise him. To see him and talk to him was very far from depressing: on the contrary, it was uplifting!

One of the joys of a Memorial Service is that, as we expose the works of him who has gone, we can remember with gratitude to God how he was in his youth and prime. It is indeed a sort of resurrection! One can forget those tired, bent legs and remember when they were strong and straight. For me those memories go back to 1933 when, in the King's Royal Rifle Corps in Belfast, we marched together to the exhilarating march which we shall hear played at the end of this Service: or when together we chased woodcock in the heather hills of South Uist! And I remember Martin very clearly in 1938 dancing the Reel at Gosford House, nicely tipsy, and swinging round the ball room with a small boy attached to each arm!

There is a bit of symbolism in that. Martin always had a genius with young people even when he himself was old. He liked them, and they loved him as he initiated them into the ways of life – not by any means excluding the best ways of getting the better of the bookmakers! He was probably the finest trainer of equerries there has been for generations! And, of course, it was not only the young he was good with: he was marvellously good with people of every age and condition and one reason why he was so good was that in dealing with people he had absolutely no side: he had the gift of making every person he talked to believe that he or she was, for him, the most important person in the world.

Many will remember with gratitude being instantly put at ease on their arrival at Clarence House or Royal Lodge and having a fortifying drink pressed into their hands. And I may say that dear Martin was as generous in dispensing his own alcohol as he was in pouring out Queen Elizabeth's! The parties he gave to his brother Officers each autumn before the Regimental dinner are unforgettable.

Martin was, of course, a bit of an actor, but behind that theatricality was a person of sensitive feeling, a shrewd observer with a critical sense and a warm heart. Like the best of people who have no children of their own, Martin found satisfaction and fulfilment in his family, particularly his beloved Sister and her children, and in his many friends; and though he never married, he loved women and women loved him. Martin sometimes said he as 'a loner', but he wasn't because he genuinely minded about other people. Although with most people he hid his real feelings beneath a cloak of jokes and laughter, with a few, perhaps a very few, he fully understood the meaning and joys of intimacy.

In many ways Martin was a secret person who did not wear his heart on his sleeve, and one of the periods of which he spoke little was his time as a prisoner of War. Perhaps he wished to put it behind him. Captured at Calais in 1940 he remained a prisoner until the Armistice.

But he was not a passive prisoner! He escaped four times but was recaptured and eventually he received the accolade awarded to the most troublesome prisoners of being incarcerated at Colditz. Before Colditz he took part in the daring and dangerous 'Wire job at Warburg' and was free for three weeks before being recaptured. He tunnelled his way out of Eichstadt but was again recaptured. And when he wasn't escaping he proved himself to be a fine leader by keeping up other prisoners' morale; he never appeared depressed or over-excited: indeed he came to prominence in the Camps because of his irrepressible good spirits. He was NOT an inveterate or obvious baiter of the guards but his quieter, more subtle approach in ribbing them was every bit as effective. And Martin managed throughout to look like an Officer with his tall and erect figure impressively nonchalant even in torn and dirty battledress!

After the war, Martin found employment in the Far East and in Australia in the service of Admiral Mountbatten, Malcolm Macdonald and Field-Marshal Slim, who had a particularly high opinion of him. He ran their households and organised their public engagements and learnt in the process many of the skills which were later to make him such a brilliant Private Secretary to Queen Elizabeth.

As well as having notable charm, Martin was a highly efficient Staff Officer. He had an excellent memory for people, a firm grasp of detail, courage, humour and, when necessary, the ability to show daring initiative. There is a story of him during his time with Malcolm Macdonald in Singapore which illustrates some of these qualities in a dramatic way.

One evening the young King of Thailand and his beautiful Queen came to dinner at Government House, and things began in a rather sticky fashion because the unfortunate King was tense and shy – a fact that Queen Sirikit whispered apologetically into Martin's ear. Martin decided he must take some action to break the tension and get the party going and, drawing on his store of knowledge and on his courage, said to the King:

'Your Majesty, rumour has it that you are extremely good at standing on your head: do please show us how you do it.'

The King was delighted at the invitation, immediately demonstrated his considerable acrobatic skill by standing on his head and, from that moment on, the party went like a wedding bell!

I hope with all my heart that the story is true: but I have no reason to believe that Queen Elizabeth knew of it when in 1956 she invited Martin to join her household! It was at any rate an inspired appointment, both for Her Majesty and for Martin. To quote P.G. Wodehouse, Martin fitted into the job 'like a prawn into aspic'!

He served Her Majesty with loyalty, love and skill from the moment of his appointment until the very day of his death. And, of course, for Martin it was much more than 'just a job'. It was for him a life in which he found fulfilment and satisfaction far beyond what most people can hope to find in their working lives.

He had a special love for the Castle of Mey and was able to help Queen Elizabeth with her racing because he loved racing and knew a great deal about it. Even when he was getting older and less well physically he said that whatever else he had to give up, he would retain his interest in Queen Elizabeth's horses. He was much loved on the race course. He was also much loved in the world of the theatre where he got a great deal of fun out of backing certain productions. He lived for many years in Hertfordshire where his family had been for generations and there too he was much loved.

I like to think also that he got a great deal of satisfaction in helping to organise Queen Elizabeth's joyous annual visits to Eton College where he had many friends and admirers. He would, I am sure, be glad to know that the Eton Boating Song is to be played at the end of this Service as well as his Regiment's Regimental March.

Let us now, in this Church of St. Martin's in the Fields, remember him and his works with praise and thanksgiving. As we hear the

Last Post and the Reveille blown on the silver Bugle, let us thank God for his life, and the fun of knowing him – for his courage, fortitude and faith at the end, for his friendship and the love he gave, for his true and faithful service to his Queen, his Country and to Queen Elizabeth: let us say with full and grateful hearts –
Thanks be to God.

LADY MARGARET COLVILLE

Meg Egerton, as she was before she married, was born in 1918, the daughter of the 4th Earl of Ellesmere. She and I became friends when we were both debs together. Our families were connected through marriage, her father having been at Eton with my father. Grenfells, Lambtons and Bulteels were all old friends and shared interests and enthusiasms for every form of horse sport. Not that any of this was shared by Meg and me. We seemed just to enjoy each other's company and laughed at the same things and got on well. She would come and stay with us when we lived in Wales before the War. Once, coming back to London by car driven by my brother Harry on a hot Whitsun Bank holiday, we decided to stop and buy an ice cream off a Walls stall . . . Meg was appalled at such an idea. To our astonishment she had never been allowed to do such a thing before. We persuaded her it was quite all right and she seemed to enjoy it.

I used to be equally amazed when I went to tea with her at her parents' vast London house, Bridgewater House, next to St James's Palace, when I was shown through a hall hung with huge Titians. I found that awesome.

She was one of that generation who were catapulted by the war from a sheltered and spacious background into another world. In spite of this childhood, in a large family of sisters and one brother, later the Duke of Sutherland, spent between Bridgewater House and Mertoun in the Scottish borders, Meg took the new social order in her stride. After doing the London Season as a popular debutante, a short time before the war she enlisted with her life-long friend Celia Doriel (who later married William, Lord Whitelaw) in the Army Territorial Service (A.T.S) both as Privates.

Meg decided not to tell her parents until called up. When they were told, her father's only stipulation was that she should have her uniform made by his London tailor. After a spell of training at the Edinburgh Command HQ, Meg worked as a clerk. She was then put forward for promotion and appeared in front of a selection board. She was asked: 'Where did you go to school?' She answered that she had never been to school. 'Do you play hockey?' – No, she did not play hockey. They asked a spate of questions to which all the answers were similarly negative. They asked her what she did do? Meg said 'I type all the morning, and wipe out what I've typed all afternoon.'

The board, to her humiliation, began to laugh and Meg, red in the face, told an anxious Celia: 'I don't know what I did. They are all laughing.'

She became a junior Subaltern and after a few staff jobs

was sent to the Orkeys for two years, a fairly grim outpost at the time and far removed from the social life that had been hers. Meg found herself dealing with a company of girls with welfare problems which she never knew could or did exist. Yet, always fascinated by human nature, a natural listener and compassionate without being sentimental, Meg's many talents were developed and she ended the war with a lot of experience.

Always one to tell self-deprecating stories, Meg told of her part in the Victory Parade in Prince's Street in Edinburgh at the end of the war. Given command to march at the head of an ATS column, Meg, who in her youth was used to country walks, set off at a brisk pace, only to glance round when half-way down the street to realise her column was almost out of sight behind her.

In 1946 she was appointed a lady-in-waiting to the then Princess Elizabeth. To this new job she brought all her skills. Not only did she have impeccable family connections, but she had an easy and quick ability to get on and connect with everyone, however fleeting the meeting might be. She was a perfectionist and having learnt the hard way, she was an extremely efficient worker in the lady-in-waitings' office. She never abandoned a task until all the ends were tied up and everything completed, however many hours it might take.

In her private life, Meg was immaculate too, in her houses, and she loved her clothes, which were always perfect for whatever occasion. She would think nothing of shopping all day in London in search of the right button!

Likewise Meg was an enjoyer of life. There were very few parties or occasions when she did not find some point and always saw the funny side of life.

In 1948 Meg was taken by the Royal Family on their epic tour of South Africa where she met John Colville and they married in 1949. Both Jock and she left their courtier jobs almost immediately after marriage. Jock returned to the Foreign Office and Meg and he were sent on various foreign postings, where she again added to her stock of friends, always somehow managing to keep up with them. During this time they had three children, two sons and a daughter. Her devotion to her family was pivotal to her existence.

Both she and Jock were friends of the Queen Mother and stayed every year at Birkhall, so after she became a widow (in 1987) it seemed an obvious choice that she be appointed (in 1990) an extra lady-in-waiting to the Queen Mother. Meg was then in her seventies and hoped she might make the *Guinness Book of Records* as the oldest-ever appointed lady-in-waiting.

It was a brilliant appointment. She not only went far back in the Queen Mother's life, not least because of the South African Tour, thus sharing many memories, but her sense of fun matched the Queen Mother's and whenever she was at Clarence House the place reverberated with their laughter. Meg continued to be as conscientious as ever, mastering the programmes and dealing with every sort of guest. When letters poured into Clarence House on the Queen Mother's birthdays, it fell to the ladies-in-waiting to answer them and Meg would work behind the scenes for weeks signing letters of reply.

Her devotion could get her into trouble. On being called for an unexpected duty at the weekend from London, she decided she needed a long evening dress from her Hampshire house.

It was a Saturday and, though offered a chauffeur-driven car, she spurned it as being mean to the chauffeur, drove herself, got late and began to drive back to Royal Lodge in the failing light. She took a wrong turn off the motorway and hit a lamp-post hard enough to describe it afterwards as looking like a banana.

Though hurt herself, she refused help from either an ambulance or the police, but gratefully accepted the spontaneous offer of rescue from a kind man with a white van. The two of them scooped up her belongings strewn round her car (which was a write-off), and she prevailed on him to drive her to Royal Lodge. She had not noticed the logo on his van. He duly swept up to the front door of Royal Lodge and she stepped out, to the astonishment of the footman waiting to receive her. The van was emblazoned with 'Help the Aged'. Meg made the most of this story and ignored the fact that she was hurt until the weekend party was over.

The sudden and short illness that ended with her death seemed curiously out of character. She had always been so full of life, ready for adventure and, only a fortnight before, had been sightseeing in Amsterdam. She was planning a visit to

Russia. She lit up the lives of her family and friends. She was a great laugher and she cheered people up whenever she was there.

LADY ELIZABETH BASSET

Elizabeth Basset came into my life when we were both ladies-in-waiting to the Queen Mother. She was an older and always wise friend of enormous value. I think initially we were a bit puzzled by each other as our lives had taken very different courses, but we both came from a family of sisters. Elizabeth's only brother, who was killed in the war, I had known slightly on the dance floor. I had also known her younger sister as a fellow deb. But I soon discovered that if you became a friend of Elizabeth you had something special. You became involved in a circle of people of all descriptions from Benedictine monks to writers and artists.

She provided me with one of the most enjoyable jobs in Queen Elizabeth's gift. Queen Elizabeth was Patron of the Royal Foundation of St Katherine in the East End. It is a foundation which was created by Queen Matilda in the 15th century and since then its patron has always been the Queen Consort when available. As might be imagined it has a fascinating history and tradition. When the Queen Mother needed someone to represent her on the Council she naturally turned to Elizabeth. In spite of having had many contacts with them over the years, it was characteristic of her generosity

Elizabeth suggested me. It was an assignment I much enjoyed. When Elizabeth died, I wrote this tribute to her:

Elizabeth Basset was quintessentially "a friend for all seasons". Those who will mourn her will be from all walks of life, and will include many who will only know her through her published anthologies, which have brought comfort and understanding to a wide readership.

People who met Elizabeth even fleetingly commented on how her goodness shone through. To her friends this was an essential part of her character. During her long years of devoted and faithful service as lady-in-waiting to the Queen Mother, she made friends with a wide spectrum of people. Her love of music and poetry, a recognition of, and enjoyment in artists in all forms led to friendships with many of them, such as Ted Hughes, the Poet Laureate, whom she met on regular fishing visits to Scotland. She would comment on the wisdom she had imbibed from such friends, but remained unselfconsciously and humbly unaware of the insight and wisdom they had been given by her. She always had time and compassion for everyone, but treated every person like an exciting discovery, to be listened to, to be encouraged, to enjoy and be laughed with. She evoked devotion and gave devotion in unmeasured quantities.

Elizabeth's spirituality was the core of her being. Worship, prayer, contemplation and meditation were essential for her. She never proselytised or preached, it was just a source of her loneliness, her beauty and truth.

This enriched her participation in ordinary life. As a previous owner she loved racing and horses, a good gossip, a good party, theatres, operas, concerts were all grist to her mill. Her loyalty, fun and funniness where her enduring contributions as a colleague and her irresistible sense of humour and sense of the ridiculous spun a thread through all this. Pomposity was quite alien to her but dignity she honoured. Elizabeth was a life enhancer and enjoyer.

Elizabeth compiled five anthologies, which proved a great help to those who read them at times of crisis during their lives. *Beyond the Blue Mountains* addressed questions of living and dying. Ted Hughes, the Poet Laureate, described it as 'a great schooling in the department of the human spirit at the ultimate confrontation,' and Dame Cicely Saunders, founder of the Hospice movement, wrote that it would 'help those who have few words of their own to find new meaning and hope.'

When my granddaughter, Laura, was killed by a crocodile while swimming in a reputedly safe waterhole in Africa, I wrote these words which were read at a service of thanksgiving for her in Lochawe in May 1996. Elizabeth included them in *Beyond the Blue Mountains*:

A Time to Mourn and a Time to Dance
A Prayer for Laura

We are here to give thanks for Laura. To try to ease the pain for our loss by remembering all her ways.

How she was joyous, full of happiness and always alert to see and appreciate the funniness in life; and to resolve its discords with an endearing frankness.

How she grew up to love her independence and making her own choices. How she equally loved her homecoming, sharing her experiences, her adventures and her jokes.

How she had the exuberance and zest of youth, grasped life and all it offered her, especially in her love of art, music, acting and writing.

How she worked so loyally, caringly and imaginatively at school and at home through her sense of service to her causes.

How she loved fun, dancing, parties and friends.

How she was full of wonder, anticipation, trust and fearlessness.

How she laughed so often and comforted us, and was our peacemaker.

Lord may we always remember her, be thankful for the gift of her and the beauty of her young life.

JOYCE GRENFELL 1910-1979

Joyce would have been 100 this year. She was my first sister-in-law, the first outsider to penetrate our close family circle and widen its circumference. To a pair of small sisters at the tail end of that family that was quite an experience. It had never occurred to them that any of their elder brothers or sisters would marry. That was something only grown-ups did; from their view at the age of nine and eleven, it was a happening as remote as dying.

It must have been daunting for Joyce to be faced with this new family. In-laws usually require a bit of absorbing, and these were numerous and varied. My mother (Reggie's step-mother) needs a dozen pens to describe her; she was a strong-willed lady, if rather eccentric. Joyce acquired a brother-in-law, and no fewer than five sisters-in-law.

One thing my mother never excelled at, or tried to excel at, was handing on to her daughters any clothes sense, or even advice on the sheer practicalities of life. Clothes for the youngest members of the family were either bought in frantic Saturday morning shopping sessions in Harvey Nichols, where two of everything was chosen, or concocted from yards of unlikely and strange material sent to any old dressmaker, probably picked because she was a starving refugee. It all ended in two little girls being poured into the same outfit, one thin and one fat, both feeling self-conscious and furious.

Joyce was immediately recognised wholeheartedly, and no doubt with relief by our mother as one who knew about 'those things' and who was interested in them. Dressing alike came to an end. Quite often Joyce took on the shopping expeditions and chose the materials and the dressmaker. Buying clothes became an exciting pleasure.

Joyce was soon an authority to appeal to. She always respected the imagination of children and treated them with that rare gift which made them feel grown up as if they were contemporaries. So fascination, surprise, and a fresh world of romance and gaiety were our first impressions of our new sister. Almost imperceptibly the songs sung round the piano changed from 'The Lass of Richmond Hill' and 'Early one morning' to the latest current popular successes. With these came the stories and the mimics and the characters.

Sitting round the drawing room fire in the evening, in the family home in Wales in pre-television days, urged on by the children, Joyce would start a character. Shirl and her boyfriend Norm came early, in a lot of different guises, and there was the nervous debutante making inane conversation, and an old character who used Joyce's special 'mouth', with tongue folded over the bottom teeth. Often the events had actually happened during the day and were re-lived through the eyes of these imaginary people. In a way, when she first made them public, a tiny bit of our family audience almost resented them being so exposed. They were such a real world in young imaginations.

Joyce became forever the family's expert and arbitrator in all matters sartorial. When she was young, she was fashionable; unlike her in-laws she did not leave her clothes to chance. She rarely wore anything severe and I can never remember her in black; something always flowed, and there was softness and colour. The dresses she designed for her own wedding were glamorous and romantic; bridesmaids in white velvet with long medieval sleeves lined with green velvet.

At family weddings Joyce was usually dressing the bride, adjusting a veil or a wreath, and even occasionally despatching a recalcitrant bridesmaid to have her hair seen to. Her confederate on these occasions was Minnie, our nanny, who admired and approved of Joyce's expertise and orderliness in organising this side of the proceedings. It was not surprising that Joyce figured so much at family weddings, as she was a romantic in its best sense: in her love of beauty and harmony and her expectation of happy endings.

It also fell to Joyce to help and advise the sisters-in-law in a lot of practical details. She was acutely aware of the agonies teenagers go through, when embarrassments can become crises. It was she who gave me deodorant and face powder, and I can even remember an early lipstick called Tangee, which I was sure for a long time was the last word in sophistication. Once, when nervously sitting in a train, thinking of the possible pitfalls facing me at the weekend party I was en route for, I heard the sound of running feet coming down the platform. It was my mother; she pressed a small parcel into my hand saying breathlessly 'Joyce gave it to me. Use very, very little, and never tell your father.' It was a small tin of rouge.

Joyce threw herself with enthusiasm into any project which involved decorating a house. She and her mother-in-law had merging tastes. Their sense of colour and light was very similar; both liked a measure of simplicity – not for them elaborate flower arrangements, flounces where controlled, rooms lit by lamps not ceiling lights. They always took genuine pleasure in each other's homes and frequently used each other's ideas. The flower table in Joyce's flat originated in a family house.

The sadness began when the realization came that Reggie and Joyce were probably not going to have children; this tragedy took some time to be absorbed. Then, most surprisingly, a lifeline was thrown to Joyce by Herbert Farjeon, the producer of reviews. He told her he would give her a chance to appear on the stage. At first Joyce was reluctant to take this step, but Reggie persuaded her there was nothing to lose.

Her almost immediate rise to stardom startled both of them and us. Joyce found opposition in the form of extreme disapproval on the part of her aunt, Lady Astor. Nor was it entirely welcomed by my parents as, according to their lights, it was not respectable to become an actress. Much later on she had a part in a film and we went to see it when it was shown in

Leicester Square. Queuing for the bus at Piccadilly afterwards my father who had a penetrating loud voice suddenly said 'I do wish Joyce would not . . . especially in Leicester Square.' It rather surprised the queue. But it was typical of Joyce over the next few years to hone this gift by hard work and self-discipline of a high order so that she turned herself from what Noël Coward had first described, much to her annoyance, as a talented amateur. This description she soon dealt with by becoming a consummate professional.

Joyce was one of the most generous people I have ever known. As her and Reggie's fortune progressed, they gave considerable sums to all of us and although childless themselves contributed to the education of other people's offspring. It was not only the family they gave to but many friends benefited as well. Joyce was an intensely loyal person both as a relation and as a friend. When she got fan mail from totally unknown people she would conscientiously answer every one and often ended up having lengthy correspondence with them. She loved people and spent a lot of her time on the top of buses and other places listening to people. Often they told her their stories. This resulted in her taking on as a friend a totally unknown old man for whom she provided comforts and visiting him in hospital for several years until he died.

Reggie became the director of a copper mine in South Africa and would go out there every winter with Joyce. It was at the time of apartheid of which Joyce was a rigorous opponent and one of her best sketches was based on a conversation with her black driver, telling her what books meant to him. Having no means to travel the world himself, he lived through his reading experiences. Although most of Joyce's sketches were comic this is one of her rare serious numbers and amongst her very best.

It does not seem possible that this year, 2010, is the centenary of Joyce's birth. Joyce certainly died too young, but it is difficult to think of her as a truly old lady. Even in her last few years, when she was sorely troubled by the loss of one eye, she was still energetic and gave great pleasure when she appeared on the television programme, *Face the Music*. She had an enormous spread of friends all over the world from Australia to Hollywood and many other places. Her memorial service in Westminster Abbey was attended by over 2,000 people, many of whom did not know her personally but somehow felt she was a friend.

Amongst the letters of condolence Reggie received was one saying 'I remember reading something by David Hockney, when he heard the news that Picasso was dead. He went to Christopher Isherwood and said "Picasso has died." Isherwood said: "Oh has he? That's not like him". I think that Joyce would have liked that said about her.'

VIRGINIA'S COMMON PLACE BOOK

Virginia Thesiger was Joyce's lifelong friend. They wrote to each other every day if they were away, and rang each other up every morning when they were both in London. Their letters took the form of a diary and they both kept them over the years. When they died they were found meticulously sorted, ready for publication. Janie Hampton edited these letters and they detail their lives in every way.

Virginia also became a friend of the family's. Virginia's father was Harry Graham, a well-known lyricist himself. At one point in the 1930s, he was writing the lyrics for several successful London musicals simultaneously. He was famous for his books of *Ruthless Rhymes for Heartless Homes*, a collection of black humour poems. He was compared to W.S. Gilbert, Edward Lear, and Hilaire Belloc, as well as being an early influence on P.G. Wodehouse.

Amongst the songs he wrote and for which he became world famous, were: 'You are my heart's delight', the music for which was composed by Franz Lehar. It was sung by the very famous tenor Richard Tauber. He also wrote 'Goodbye' in the musical, *The White Horse Inn*, for which royalties come in to this day.

On the occasion when Kaiser Wilhelm went to Brussels and was said to have spoken to the Curator of the Congo Museum in three languages, Harry Graham imagined the conversation. It might perhaps be relevant to-day in Brussels?

'Guten Morgan, mon ami'
'Heute is es schone wetter'
'Charme de vous voir ici'
'Never seen you looking better'.

Virginia used to write entertaining little poems for us. When King George V was recovering from his serious illness in 1928, he went to Bognor to recuperate. He honoured it by giving it the accolade of Regis. I can remember a catchy rhyme which Virginia wrote then.

I used to want to live on caviar
Have a bathroom to each bedroom
And a Rolls-Royce car,
But since I have fell for you
I'll be content to share
Your bungalow at
Bognor Regis.

Virginia collected quotes which she kept in a common place book. Peter and Celia Fleming were great friends of both Reggie and Joyce, and Virginia and her husband Tony. Celia was the celebrated actress Celia Johnson. On a postcard headed 'From Mrs Peter Fleming, Merrimoles House, Nettlebed, Oxon', is the following:

'Darling Gin. I expect you know this but I found it today and it made me laugh out loud

Song of the ballet
Lift her up tenderly
Raise her with care
Catch hold of one leg
And a handful of hair,
Swing her round savagely,

And when this palls,
Heave Ho! Away with her
Into the stalls . . .

Love from Celia

In the winter of 1979, known as the winter of discontent there was quite a circulation for this one:

The Lord said to Noah: 'Where is the Ark I commanded you to build?' And Noah said: 'Verily I have had three carpenters off sick. The gopher wood supplier hath let me down – yea even though the gopher wood hath been on order for nigh on 12 months. The damp-course specialist hath not turned up.'

And God said to Noah: 'I want the Ark finished before seven days and seven nights.'

And Noah said: 'It will be so.'

The Lord said to Noah: 'What seems to be the trouble this time?'

Noah said: 'My sub-contractor hath gone bankrupt. The pitch for the outside of the Ark hath not arrived. The glazier departeth on holiday to Majorca, yea even though I offered him double time. Shem hath formed a pop group with his brothers Ham and Japeth

ABOVE Vice-Admiral John Pascoe Grenfell of the Imperial Brazilian Navy 1800-1869. The painting, made after June 1852, shows Grenfell wearing the Order of the Rose awarded for the Battle of Tonelero 1851, and above it the Imperial Order of the Southern Cross. He was made a full Admiral in 1863 and retired in 1864. (The painting is in the care of the Parker family).

ABOVE Maria Dolores Masini married Admiral John Pascoe Grenfell. My paternal great-grandmother.

BELOW Jane Lawley with her parents, Lord and Lady Wenlock. My maternal great-grandmother.

ABOVE Sophia Grenfell, my grandmother, 1834-1898.

ABOVE RIGHT General Sir Neville Lyttelton, my maternal grandfather.

RIGHT My mother, Hilda Margaret Grenfell.

Martin Gilliat and Frances Campbell Preston outside Martin's cottage at Welwyn.

Lady Margaret Colville.

Lady Elizabeth Basset.

H.M. The Queen Mother on her 80th birthday with her household, from left to right – Ashe Windham, Ralph Anstruther, Ruth Fermoy, Elizabeth Grimthorpe, Katherine Abercorn, Martin Gilliat, Olivia Mulholland, Simon Dalhousie, Elizabeth Basset, John Griffin, Frances Campbell-Preston and Alistair Aird.

LEFT Joyce and Reggie 1935.

BELOW Virginia and Joyce on holiday in Venice, 1949.

RIGHT Mrs Alington (Aunt Hester) and C.A. Alington.

BELOW Hermione Hichens with, from left to right, John (killed in Normandy 1944), Stella (Mrs Hornby), Mark and Phoebe (Mrs Pearce).

Minnie Barnes with the author, 1918.   Charles Ian Fraser of Reelig.

Ardchattan Priory.

. . . Lord I am undone.'

The Lord grew angry and said: 'What about the animals, two of every sort I have ordered to come to be kept alive. Where for example are the giraffes?'

And Noah said: 'They have been delivered to the wrong address, but should arrive on Friday.' And the Lord said: 'Where are the monkeys and the elephants and the zebras?'

And Noah said: 'They are expected to-day.'

The Lord said to Noah: 'How about the unicorns?' Noah wrung his hands and wept: 'O Lord, Lord, they are

a discontinued line. Thou canst not get unicorns for love or money. Thou knowest how it is?'

And the Lord said: 'Noah my son, I know. Why doest thou think I have caused a flood?'

The next two quotes speak for themselves:

Dear Mr and Mrs Trimble

God bless you for giving your old radio to the Community Chest, which in turn gave it to me. I have lived here in this nursing home since my dear husband passed away 12 years ago. I am 87 years old and never have any visitors so I get lonesome. Mrs Rogers who lives in the next room is 89 and she has had a radio since she came here 5 years ago but she would never let me listen to it.

Yesterday her radio fell to the ground and broke, so she asked if she could listen to mine and I said: Fuck you.

Yours sincerely

Maude Davis

Lastly from the *Wiltshire Times and Chippenham News* 1963:

Mr Harris has asked us to point out a number of inaccuracies in our story. After returning from India, he served in Ireland for four years and not six months as stated: he never farmed at Heddington, particularly not at Coate Road Farm as stated; he has never counted cycling or walking among his hobbies; he is not a member of 54 hunts; and he did not have an eye removed at Chippenham hospital after an air raid . . .

Virginia may well have had as good a talent as her father, but she never really developed it. Her writing was always natural and pleasing but never an output that really tested her. But she was theatre critic for *The Spectator* for a number of years and she wrote for several magazines throughout her life, starting with *Punch*.

One of the reasons that she never wrote enough was that she had sufficient income all her life, but also because her husband, Tony, fell ill soon after the Second World War, suffering from premature dementia. She was his carer for a long time. After Tony's death, she wrote a touching poem:

> After so long, so long
> In my tight prison
> With my familiar shackles
> Heavy on head and heart
> After so long, so long
> Suddenly I see the bars
> With the eyes God gave me
> And suddenly, suddenly
> (Oh my heart flies out of the dream
> Like a singing bird)
> Suddenly there is freedom.

Virginia was a considerable poet and a lot of her creative talent went into helping Joyce and writing a lot of her monologues and lyrics for her. Reggie and Ginnie were Joyce's toughest critics and she was always involved.

VICTORIAN AUNTS

A n old saying asserts that God chooses your relations but you choose your friends. Personally I find I have little argument with God who made a pleasing choice on many counts on my behalf. One of these was His choice of aunts. Mine was an eclectic collection, nice and various. Some were fringe characters who nevertheless produced children or grandchildren who were relations as well as friends.

Aunts have a special place in the family establishment, as near as parents, but with a different view of events, and inevitably bringing further wisdom from their different experiences, even translating your parents to you.

My aunts started their lives as Victorians, moved on to be Edwardians, became Georgians, two of them living on to be Elizabethans. They started off in a life of transport by horses, changed to cars, later even air. They moved from candlelight and a little gas to electricity. They met the wireless and found the telephone quite practical and of use in ordinary life; apart from these startling changes and colonial wars which brought casualties to their young lives, they lived through two world wars. This to me is remarkable. Having lived through one,

I cannot imagine the agony it must have been to know you faced a re-run. They did emerge eccentric – a lovable trait and God bless them for that.

My paternal aunt, Dolores Maria Masini Grenfell, was born in 1860, the eldest sister of a family of 13. She must have known her one-armed grandfather John Pascoe, who died when she was nine, but, sadly, never told us anything about him. In her thirties she went to a Physiognomic Institute in Brighton with a business manager called Harold Dana. He analyzed her character: "She has a limited medium sized brain in which the intellectual faculties preponderate over the animal propensities" (which must have been good news). He continued in frank vein admitting that she was "naturally refined" and disliked any show "of vulgarity or exhibition of slovenliness, laziness or neglect. Her perceptive power is keen enough for all ordinary purposes though she is by no means penetrating in her observations However her intuition is good – she is able to deduce with considerable accuracy facts that would not come within her range of observation."

Apart from these brutal assessments of her mental prowess he did allow that although she had a hot temper she never bore resentment and had a sympathetic nature and a benevolent spirit and even stated "that she possesses more physical endurance than her appearance might indicate at first sight. Although highly strung she is by no means delicate, and she will probably suffer from dyspepsia. Care should be taken to avoid irregular meals."

This was something that continued all her life. I remember her as tolerating every other chaotic occurrence in our family life but unpunctual meals she could not abide. She would arrive for a meal in our house armed with a supply of biscuits which she would munch furiously till we all appeared, late. Her appearance was delicate. She was small with small wrists and ankles which looked as if they might snap, her thin hawk-like face never highly coloured.

I think it says a lot for my aunt that she kept this scathing document and it was found in her desk after her death in 1956 at the age of 96.

A great-niece remembers Lola having her to tea and discussing music. It was not a subject for which Lola ever received enthusiastic support from her own family. Her young twin brother wrote from Eton about "Patina," a waltz she had composed. "Lloyd says they never play waltzes in the concert but if you like he will play it at the volunteers concert (a very moderate affair and few people go). Will it do you any good if he plays it there?"

Lola kept a fitful diary, its main purpose seemingly to fill a boring day. But for all that it describes the atmosphere of family life lived in a large house in Buckinghamshire, Wilton Park, and the comings and goings of an energetic family, occasional references to books read, frequent outings to entertainments of the Primrose League, and a note to say she was now reading Lord Beaconsfield. Her conservative roots were well earthed. When she fell ill with a mysterious illness, the cure was a visit to Bath for the baths. Hers was a regime worthy of Jane Austen's day, one entry noting an afternoon of knitting. Her sister had just had a baby, the first nephew, Crocker Bulteel, and there is an entry: "have started Crocker's drawers."

Wherever we were on holiday, she would appear for a long visit. She always insisted that her bed had to be moved so that it faced north and south, otherwise she asserted she got giddy as she would be sleeping against the earth's rhythm. Anyone who travelled to hot climes was urged to sew a strip of red, white and blue colours down their spine to ward off the ferocity of the sun.

She was 56 by the time I was old enough to register anyone, and I became immediately aware that she loathed all things politically liberal, especially Lloyd George, whom she believed responsible for most the ills of the human race. She said the vote for women was an absurd idea. "Any woman worth her salt could make any man vote the way she wanted," so spoke my spinster aunt who had had a considerable hand in the upbringing of nine brothers. She never went out of doors without a sturdy smart hat. Her views on church did not synchronize with our mother's solid piety. Disloyally, we found this enjoyable. On being urged to join the church-going party of a Sunday, Lola, who was not an early riser, claimed she had been to church twice every Sunday for six weeks and was therefore in credit and had no need to go.

She believed emphatically that her family was the best. Her

grandfather had been in the Brazilian Navy. Lola retained accounts of the battles in which he took part. She would read aloud to us from a notebook carefully written up in a Victorian hand, recounting an engagement in which he had played a part. She somewhat bowdlerized this, as any mention of Cochrane was replaced by the name Grenfell. A young nephew who served with the Navy in World War II was not as impressed as no doubt he should have been, realising that the tales were over 100 years old.

The stuffing had been much knocked out of Lola in the First World War. She had largely brought up her younger twin brothers after the death of both their parents, when the boys were sixteen. They were both killed in the early days of the war. In 1920 John Buchan wrote a memoir of them, and Lola undertook the research, leaving a meticulous catalogue of every letter that they ever wrote each other. The book was a best-seller the year it was published and is still available (at a price) on Amazon. Then, in the Second World War she was bombed out of her flat.

Such aunts linger in the memory even if one has a rather objective relationship with them.

My maternal aunts were quite different. They might well have given short shrift to the Physiognomic from Brighton.

My grandmother was one of five sisters and two brothers, the children of Jem and Jane Stuart-Wortley, of whom Mary was the eldest. She was called Maimi and even after many years, it is difficult to think of her as anything else but 'Auntmaimi' in one word.

Her views on everything were didactic and unusual. In the eyes of her great-nieces she had no dress sense at all. She looked a hopeless frump, having early on refused to wear corsets "for reasons of hygiene". One of her great-nieces, Alice Buchan, wrote: "her hats were somewhat square and like footstools; her shoes were elastic-sided like a Dame in Pantomime." But she had a past that was intriguing.

By Victorian standards her family was impecunious, in spite of living just off St James' Street, London, but Auntmaimi decided she wanted to be an artist and enrolled at the Slade, the only college that would accept female students. This was a considerable undertaking as the family finances didn't stretch to allowing for any transport. Undeterred, she walked daily to Bloomsbury. Even this was dangerous as a young girl walking alone was a matter for scandal, so whenever she thought a passing carriage might contain someone she knew she had to hide as best she could.

She never became an artist (but in later life became a talented amateur architect making meticulous plans for the improvement of cottages on her husband's estates). She remained in touch with the prevailing art world and the Arts and Crafts Movement: the fixed planets in her sky being William Morris and Burne-Jones. She is depicted as one of the descending damsels who all have the same faces and figures, in the latter's painting "The Golden Staircase".

In her thirties, Auntmaimi fell in love and somewhat

mistakenly married Ralph, Lord Lovelace. When she met Ralph he was different from any other man she had known, a mountaineer, a mathematician and in his ancestry was the romantic figure of Byron, his grandfather.

She fell in love and in spite of an unhappy marriage remained so. But he was a cold and strange man frequently disappearing for days. After two years Auntmaimie returned home, only to be urged to return by her mother, who wrote to her "to keep off Season-gossip". The result was she returned and entered into what was delicately called a "Marriage Blanc".

In those days it was always easier to refer to awkward sexual situations by referring to them in French. Another aunt of the same vintage referred to a miscarriage as a "voiture manqué." Perhaps it made them sound more "proper". Ralph's consuming interest with his Byronic heredity was one she found hard to deal with.

Ralph was obsessed with the reputation of his beloved grandmother who was Byron's wife. She had been censured for divorcing him when she claimed he had had an incestuous affair with his half-sister. Lovelace felt that he could only lift the cloud of censure from her reputation by explaining his grandfather's behaviour and to set it down truthfully in a privately printed book.

Auntmaimi had no use for this Byron heredity, and thought nothing of Byron, or Lady Byron. Whenever she saw the portrait of Byron, dressed as an Albanian brigand, it caused her to show exasperation. At first her honesty and lack of cant had possibly attracted Ralph and she had hoped to divert him.

She and Ralph had one thing on which there was total agreement – they were against plumbing. It was said to waste water needed for the land by having unnecessary baths, which she also said cryptically "led to misalliances".

My sister and I were sent to stay with Auntmaimi in her extremely opulent and large house in Surrey. By then she was a widow but had been left two large estates, one at Ockham in Surrey and another in Somerset. No one had warned us of her plumbing fetish and we got a considerable fright when we pulled the plug and a deafening thud sounded. My sister thought she had killed someone until we found it was an earth closet. There was one, outstanding luxury to life at Ockham, the up-side to no plumbing. You had a hip bath. This was put in front of a blazing fire in your bedroom. Housemaids filled it up from cans of hot water and you could luxuriate in it. It was the only time in my life I ever had a hip bath, and I remember it with glowing pleasure.

Auntmaimi entertained us all her life with her firm dismissals of accepted opinions. Her views on Heaven, "It sounds awful, like an everlasting Garden Party." On going to see my grandmother in a flat in Chelsea she insisted on climbing the stairs as she "refused to trust her immortal soul to a button". At a time when sex was not encouraged amongst domestic staff, she had a distinctive view, "I really do not care how many concubines the footman has in the garage."

For all her dislike of her husband's ancestor, we liked to feel we were connected to Byron in however tenuous a way. And it certainly boosted our reading.

When looking back at the memories of these Victorian Aunts it is quaint to be writing this on a laptop in 2008. They don't seem all that far away. History goes so fast.

Hermione, my mother's younger sister, was quite different. Always a very involved aunt, she was never one to be on the fringe of life. She was a large person with great vitality and a capacity to be there whatever the situation. Good looking, without being classically beautiful, she had thick golden hair and a wide open face with blue appraising eyes. She was lovely.

She became an aunt at an early age. This is apt to make the relationship near to a sisterhood, and to my older siblings there was certainly some of this in the relationship.

Hermione led a vivid life. Like so many of her 20th century contemporaries she had times of high happiness and desperate tragedy but the strength of her character never wavered. In her early childhood her parents were stationed in South Africa where her father was serving as a General in the Boer War. A family friend was Rudyard Kipling. Coming to a meal, he found Hermione was missing from the table and enquired for her. He was told she had the chicken pox, so was sitting up a tree in the garden. He climbed the next tree to talk to her.

When her father moved on to become Commander-in-Chief in Ireland in the early 1900s, she was in her early teens and destined for a musical career. She was also an intrepid horsewoman. Years later my husband was in a prisoner-of-war camp with General Victor Fortune, who could remember affectionately riding in Phoenix Park with her. When I married into the Army in 1938, I ran into senior officers who would recollect, with doe eyes, my aunt in her teenage years. Hermione herself remembered most of Dublin's eminent society, particularly W.B. Yeats – not for his poetry but for the fact that he was extremely dirty and smelt awful.

Her life then was carefree. The Commander-in-Chief was second only to the Viceroy, and Hermione, with her two elder sisters married, was virtually his only daughter. She drove in carriage processions with her parents, she danced at balls, and had a 'golden time', as the years before the First World War were always called, and remembered by her generation.

Later my grandfather came back to London in retirement and became Governor of the Royal Hospital, Chelsea. She exchanged the Irish social scene for the London one. By 1914 she and a group of friends began to plan to train as nurses in case war happened. They signed on at a hospital as VADs (this was an auxiliary nursing unit) much to the disapproval of their parents, who expressed the wish that Hermione should not nurse any men. As she pointed out, after the first week, this was an impossible condition.

In 1914 they were sent to front line hospitals, and nursed there for the next four years. Hermione recalled arriving at a station in France, when she was returning from leave, in the early hours of the morning, without any idea where she might find a bed for the night. The year before as a young woman in London she had always been chaperoned and not even allowed to walk down Sloane Street alone.

One of her colleagues among the other nurses was Vera Brittain who, after the war, wrote "The Testament of Youth" – a heartrending account of those years. Hermione stoutly rejected her rendering, maintaining that the experience had often been entirely enjoyable, with great cameraradie, and the wonderful spirit of the patients. She would sing to them in the wards. For all her refusal to accept Vera Brittain's tragic emphasis, she wore all her life a diamond brooch given her by a grieving mother who anticipated she might have been her daughter-in-law. Whenever quizzed in later life, Hermione maintained that she probably would not have married him. Several loved cousins were killed, and however brave a face she put on afterwards, it was not part of her life she much recounted, or enjoyed recalling.

In 1920 she married Lionel Hichens a distinguished businessman, a member of the Round Table with a wide circle of friends including Lionel Curtis, Sir Edward Grigg, Lord Brand and Lord Lothian. Amongst other things he was Chairman of Cammell Lairds, the shipbuilders. Hermione took a part in instructing those invited to launch ships how they should go about it and was correspondingly disapproving if the bottle failed to break.

A totally happy period started. They had five children and a large and rambling house in Oxfordshire with a great number of rooms and spectacularly few bathrooms. Hermione inherited the family nonchalance about clothes. Fashion was not something that bothered her, or my mother either. Housekeeping was treated with similar disdain. It was practical, serviceable, but there were no frills. John Buchan maintained that Hermione wrote her letters balanced on a lampshade.

North Aston was a home from home for all of us and we took our latest young man for her to examine, unless we suspected she might not approve. So in the inter-war years the two families grew up side by side, Hermione and Lionel being rather more affluent than my family, coming often to the rescue. They gave a "coming out" dance for me. Some of the debutantes' mothers wore tiaras as was the fashion. Hermione went to Woolworth's and bought a glass one which she twined in her hair and which we thought looked very nice. Later she gave a wedding reception for us, before our economical wedding.

The Second World War brought this happy life to an end. Lionel came to London for one night during the Blitz; the building he was in was destroyed by a direct hit and he was killed. Hermione stayed on at North Aston. Now the widowed mother of a young family, she faced all the complications of trying to bring up a family, in the midst of their education, and during a war. She was supported by her eldest son John who was at Oxford and soon to join the Army. He married just before going overseas. He was killed in Normandy soon after D-Day.

This could have turned her into a tragic broken person, but not our stalwart aunt. She retrieved her gaiety and turned her post-war life into great activity. She was a County Councillor for Oxfordshire, becoming Chairman of the Education Committee, which led to enjoyable rows with other Chairmen whom she thought siphoned too much of the budget away from education. She was appointed to sit on various Government Commissions and almost invariably signed a minority report at the end. Neither she nor my mother enjoyed admitting they were wrong. They did so fairly seldom. They had little compunction about intervening in the lives of others when they were certain they knew the solution. Sometimes they won. When I went to see her in her nineties and in bed shortly before she died, she was indignant about some financial affairs of one of my sisters. She intended to right them and said: "In the spring when I can get up, you and I are going to see the bank manager." I pointed out, in vain, that we would have no right to interview my sister's bank manager. "Oh rubbish!" was the predictable answer.

Amongst her other activities was taking an almost obsessive interest in the Stock Exchange, her first thought in the morning being to get the *Financial Times* off the doorstep. She also took up farming. Her footwear became white trainers, worn on any and all occasions. She could be seen, before coming up to London for some party, dressed in her London clothes, complete with diamond brooch and pearl earrings, and white trainers, driving the tractor.

She attended cattle sales. At one such sale she planned to buy a bull and carefully marked the Lot she wanted. When the Lot came up, she started to bid with enthusiasm. The auctioneer went as far as to question her. Was she sure she was bidding for the right Lot? She was of course indignant that he should doubt her. So instead of buying a bull, she found she had bought 100 lavatory seats. When my mother telephoned her to commiserate, she got a sharp response, Hermione averring it was a shrewd buy "as the family are always wanting lavatory seats."

Amongst my Lyttelton relations was a particularly exceptional aunt. She was my grandfather's youngest half-sister, Hester. She married Cyril Alington, who became Headmaster of Eton, and Dean of Durham. She was often at the Royal Hospital, Chelsea when my grandparents lived there. We used to go down to lunch in the headmaster's house at Eton occasionally, where on one occasion we met Helen Wills Moody, then the reigning Champion at Wimbledon. I remember being fascinated by how large her hands were. There was also a story which garnered a great deal of moss as it rolled, that when Gandhi stayed with the Alingtons, he washed his teeth with a twig. Her eldest daughter, Elizabeth, married Alec Douglas-Home, who became Prime Minister and later Foreign Secretary.

Alec Douglas-Home frequently repeated some sturdy advice he received from his father-in-law. Cyril Alington told him:

"When a man says his word is as good as his bond, *always* take his bond!"

Being a close member of my mother's family Aunt Hester soon made friends with my sister-in-law Joyce Grenfell, who always referred to her as Mrs A. Joyce based one of her favourite characters "the Vice-Chancellor's wife" on Hester.

Joyce wrote a perfect tribute to her, and I can do no better than quote it:

> It is easier to say what Mrs A did not look like than to find an exact simile. She did not look like a headmaster's wife. She did not really look like a Dean's wife either. She was of course both.
>
> If you came upon her isolated from her family, she might suggest a woman gifted with gardening and highly skilled in domesticity. She looked like a mother too; one with a light hand for pastry, but she said of herself "I do not suppose there is anyone in the world more at a loss when confronted with an egg." She knew exactly what to do when confronted with a child. It was not for nothing that she headed the Mothers Union.
>
> I do not think I ever saw her looking as though her hair had been "done". I believe it used to be a wonderful Pre-Raphaelite red, but when I knew it it was a soft, pale colour but an afterglow of red remained in a faint way. She wore it piled up into a rather loosely baked bun. It never looked as if it would stay where it was for long, but I never saw it come down. She gave an impression of timelessness. She sat easy as they say in the mountains of North Carolina. She was unhurried, and that gave one a sense of space.
>
> I believe I have an observant eye, but try as I do I cannot remember what Mrs A wore. I know she had timeless kind of clothes, longer than then in fashion. I know she wore hats that went on her head and did not perch. But so powerful was the essential being inside the

clothes and the hats that they contributed little that is memorable.

She may not have been beautiful in terms of bone and complexion. Her face was broad, the cheeks high. Her eyes, that I seem to remember, as dark amber coloured, were deeply set. Her mouth was wide and mobile, and quick to smile. There emanated from her being a light, warmth and a radiance that was entirely beautiful.

Seen from the point of view of one who had known her slightly since childhood and more closely in the last 15 years of her life, she was a beloved friend and a very special person. She was individual in all she thought and said and did. She was an original.

I see her lying on the sofa in the great long-windowed room at the Deanery of Durham with its dark blue greeny Chinese wallpaper, patterned with lemon trees and white birds and pale flowers. She has the telephone on the floor beside and is working on a vast embroidered bed cover that flowed over her knees.

Some people's voices sound like strings. Hers was a combination of double bass and some deep woodwind. Her laugh was low and rich with a whisper of in-drawn breath to finish it all.

She did not go in for a strong language but "Great Lack" sufficed to relieve her feelings. She had a very individual sort of lisp. It added greatly when she emphasised, and she emphasised a lot in a completely natural way. To write down the stresses she made would make her utterances appear affected, and that was the last thing they were. They flowed out of her, unedited, inevitable and entirely unlike anyone else's.

Who else would have drawn attention in the same way to a regrettable absence of essential stationary in the visitor's bathroom?" The question of expenses came up over some concert I was doing for her, and she wrote to say "we must touch on the sordid topic of coin."

There are so many quotations. This postcard sent to a shoe shop in Sloane Street was observed on the hall table by one of the family

83

and memorised: "gently fussed over non appearance of rather dim pair of shoes sent to you for mending." Gently fussed was the exact description of the uneasy stirring it had aroused in her.

In my diary for 1948 is an entry rejoicing at being in Durham. "Mrs A is very lame but in the most blessed spirits. The white poodle has been named Mu because it is a present from the Mothers Union. She telephoned at some length to Alec and Elisabeth and called them in turn *"dear* Lord" and *"Arc Angel"*.

It is difficult to put on paper the quality of greatness that Mrs A. had .Was it her vision of heaven? This seemed to be constant and immediate. She recognised that the best in any-one was all that mattered and she had an instant awareness of this truth in quite unlikely people. She had humility. She had humour. Above all she had a sense of joy. This was no surface thing, but rather a deep-seated, golden reverberation that responded to items large and small, to miracles, to jokes, to affection, to illumination and the goodness of God. Her faith went beyond words. She gave it out, unconsciously, all the time.

She knew plenty of sorrow in her long life, but she had a wider view of life in its entirety than most of us and her courage and steadfastness went on undiminished.

My mother met an old man up in the mountains of North Carolina and they spoke of a new mutual friend who had died "he never met a stranger" said the old man. I was reminded of this when Elizabeth told me that Mrs A said "I only once met a bore". History does not relate the identity of this lone figure.

Mrs A met few strangers. She was, as an Oxford undergraduate wrote of her, "keen on heaven," and this keenness caused her to create an atmosphere of enormous joy wherever she was. There was never anybody quite like her, and to have known her is riches indeed.

I entirely agree with Joyce.

A well remembered great-aunt, Edith Lyttelton, always known as Aunt DD, was the widow of Alfred Lyttelton, my grandfather's youngest brother. He had a distinguished career both as a lawyer, became a KC, and also as a politician. He was Liberal MP for Warwick and Leamington and became Colonial Secretary. He was a well-known cricketer, and amongst many other stories, Aunt DD said he disliked wicket-keeping behind W.G. Grace, as the famous cricketer smelt so. Alfred died at the age of 56 after being struck in the stomach by a cricket ball from which he got an abscess that killed him in 1913.

He left his widow with two children. But she had a distinguished career of her own, which was rather exceptional in those Edwardians days. She was Alfred's second wife, his first wife having died tragically after a year of marriage, having a still-born baby. DD's maiden name was Balfour. She was related to Arthur Balfour, the Prime Minister. She was born in St Petersburg Russia in 1865 and was educated privately and married Alfred in 1892. She was a considerable intellectual. (I was once caught sitting between her and her daughter, Mary, on the back seat of a car driving to London, when they had a conversation about one of Jane Austen's novels which was, for me, of such erudition that I did not understand one word of it. I think it was about whether Jane Austen should have used the word 'such' as 'but' in some context, and hinged on nuances that could be made by using 'but' instead of some equal three-letter word.)

As a result of a visit to South Africa with Alfred in 1900 they became friends of Lord Milner and that resulted in her becoming a founder member of the Victoria League. She was also a founder of the Personal Service Association (founded in 1908 to alleviate distress caused by unemployment in London). During World War One she seems to have had a busy time from starting the Committee for War Refugees and ending up as a British delegate to the League of Nations in 1923. She was made a DBE in 1917 and a GBE in 1929.

DD was a friend of the actress, Mrs Patrick Campbell, and so was involved in the early stages of planning the National Theatre, a project completed by her son Oliver (Viscount Chandos) and she sat on the Executive Committee of Shakespeare Memorial Theatre. None of this really interested when we were children. She was just another character in a wide circle of relations and friends who went between our grandparents' and our family houses.

She was a large figure and immensely friendly with feet firmly on the ground which gave her a look of stability and safety to children, and we were extremely fond of her. For of all her exceptional achievements, she was not a remote person but she invoked in us an instinctive trust. She was a friend of Lady Astor's and was a natural person for my sister Laura to tug the hand of to stop Lady Astor from making an unfortunate scene at the rehearsal for Joyce and Reggie's wedding.

In my memory none of my Lyttelton aunts are remembered

as having individual clothes. They are all dressed in variations of black dresses decorated by the odd diamond brooch and pearls with hats plonked on their heads with probably another diamond brooch lodged somewhere on the hat, and sensible shoes. There was a story of one of my grandmother's friends who wrote to her dressmaker a postcard saying 'same dress as before please.' Into this category Aunt DD fitted exactly.

After Alfred died, she became involved and interested in Psychical Research. This was very much connected to her family, as in 1888 Gerald Balfour, Arthur Balfour's younger brother, along with a group of scientists, classical scholars, and philosophers, had founded the Institute for Psychic Research, later to transmogrify into the College of Physchic Science, which exists to this day.

When I was in my teens, DD used to ask me to her country cottage. An inveterate matchmaker, my aunt encouraged one particular young man to take an interest in me. He was a nice austere man, who was interested in her theories. Later he appeared in my husband's prisoner-of-war camp and was among the very few people who made a successful escape. When he got back to London, I came down from Scotland hoping to see him. But the security authorities banned him from seeing anyone so we never met again. We often spoke about him later.

My aunt used to regale me with another complicated story. It concerned Alfred's sister May, who had died of typhoid in her 20s. It was said that she and Arthur Balfour had been on the point of getting engaged. In those days the cure for typhoid was to shave off the patient's hair. This was done to May, but her heartbroken nanny collected up her tresses, put them in a box and gave them to Arthur Balfour. This arrangement was secret between him and the nanny and no one else knew anything about it.

Amongst the founders of the Society were some who made a pact that those who died first would get a message back to prove they were still able to communicate. After a while a mysterious number of events began to happen. Mediums all over the world began to get strange messages in a language eventually proving to be classical Greek. In time these messages came through a well-established London medium with a double name known to the College and the Balfour family. It appeared to be aimed at Arthur Balfour and referred to a casket with hair. Bingo! Aunt DD told me that careful research and checking had been undertaken for many years. By the time she told me this siory, Arthur Balfour and all the participamts had been long dead. But DD assured me that when the final facts had been verified and published (she was speaking in the 1930s), no-one could doubt the fact of the after life. I aquired a copy in the 1970s and was suitably impressed. I leant it to a mutual cousin who said he'd never read such codswallop in his life and either lost it or burnt it.

It was quite an eclectic collection of aunts and I feel lucky to have been able to claim relationship with them. No wonder I enjoyed my childhood.

MINNIE BARNES

According to some of the best journalistic brains, if you had a nanny you are 'Posh' or a 'Toff'. Minnie Barnes was our nanny and would have found this a comic description of us. She nurtured and loved us as we loved her for the half century we had the luck to spend together, in many different circumstances. Her memory is treasured by me, my children and grandchildren, nephews and nieces, and equally by numerous other members of the family.

Minnie was born in Herefordshire as one of a large family, but her father was killed in an accident when the children were all young and her mother had a hard struggle raising them all. Minnie herself always wanted to be a nurse, but it was a profession that was hard to get into without financial backing. So she went into domestic service at the age of 14 with an elderly couple who were friends of my Lyttelton grandparents.

Early on Minnie made her mark, as was characteristic of the rest of her life, and she became, at a young age, lady's maid to her employer. When the couple died, they left Minnie a small amount of money which she carefully guarded for the rest of her life. Also, fortunately for us, she was immediately employed by my mother as her lady's maid.

Minnie's talents were many. She was a beautiful seamstress and the christening robe she made for me is still brought out for use as new generations appear. She was a green-fingered gardener and became a high class cook. My father, who was something of a gourmet, and went to Paris for its food, said she was the best cook of game birds he had ever known. All through their lives they were allies. Minnie could, and did turn herself into many different roles as family fortunes fluctuated. After the First World War when my sister Laura and I became 'after-thought' babies in the family, Minnie became our nanny, on condition she was never addressed as 'Nanny' but remained 'Minnie', so we two had a special relationship with her. Mostly our mother and Minnie pulled together regarding our welfare, but as we grew up and Minnie's function as nanny diminished, so she took on other functions, and her relationship with my mother didn't run so smoothly, ending, sadly, during the stesses of the London blitz in a total rupture.

Minnie was always practical and they needed space to operate sensibly together. The overcrowded basement flat put paid to that. Minnie would get up at a very early hour to go to some remote district to buy the family rations at street markets, which were both cheaper and fresher, a point never appreciated by my mother. When the rift finally came, Minnie moved over to come and look after my baby, and after that, she split her life between Laura and me, cosseting us in whatever way she thought most useful, perhaps cooking for Laura in her

London flat after the war, at a time when Laura showed little inclination to want to marry, saying that she would never be so comfortable again in her life.

I don't think Minnie's life ever reached its possible potential. Had she succeeded in becoming a nurse when she was young, she would almost certainly have become an influential Matron somewhere. She was an organizer and softened the impact of changes in our houses and 'life-styles' by managing, behind the scenes, in the kitchen so that there was seldom if ever a fuss if anyone suddenly brought unexpected guests. She kept her hand on organizing the untrained other staff who would appear from different charities backed by either my mother or sister Vera. She was not daunted when terrified orphans arrived from Dr Barnardo's at 14, and they always remained friends of Minnie's when they inevitably moved on to better themselves, thanks to her training.

She had her very distinct views on life. She never fancied the Church going encouraged, not to say forced, by our mother. Wherever we landed up, my mother made tender enquires as to whether Minnie had found a local church she would like to go to? Minnie always had a dead pat answer that there were none that fulfilled her present religious leanings.

Her political views veered. After the Second World War she voted Labour, explaining that much as she admired Mr Churchill, she had found during her life that boys were apt to get swollen headed if admired for too long. But her Labour leanings got a jolt. She had decided to retire when, after the death of her sister, her brother-in-law, a prosperous coal-merchant, asked her to live with him. This arrangement was ideal but suddenly her brother-in-law died. After his death Minnie discovered he had failed to cash in his pension for several weeks, so she went to get it, to be told as he was dead she couldn't have it. In vain she pointed out that he had at the time been alive. It finished her belief in the Welfare state, as she was sure this was a ruse of the Cabinet, and possibly Mr Attlee personally, to pinch the savings of the poor.

She returned to live with Patrick and me in Scotland at the time when the Government announced a free tobacco allowance for all old age pensioners. Minnie strongly disapproved of smoking but nonetheless insisted on collecting her ration every week, convinced that if she didn't, the Cabinet would once more benefit. It was quite a chore, living as we did several miles from a post office. She even refused to give or sell this loot to us, and periodically she held a ritual bonfire of tobacco in the garden. At the next Election, she voted Conservative.

She never achieved empathy with the Scots. I found her fuming one day after ringing the milkman who had failed to deliver the milk, but had reassured her by saying it would arrive 'back of the mid-day.' She was furious. Which was 'the back of the mid-day'? – before or after? Minnie was quintessentially English.

Thrift was important to her and it extended to conservation. One of the mysteries of her life was how she found space in which to store the things she chose to save. To travel with her was interesting as she would appear to have a perfectly ordinary hand bag, but it contained everything and we thought for some reason was bottomless. She could produce anything needed from a screwdriver to a pack of cards, aspirins or apples. After years of tryng as children to catch her out we always failed.

She never achieved a room to herself until quite late on in life, usually sharing with one of the babies or another member of the staff. So it was a surprise when a whole tea-set, rescued from the debris when the Royal Hospital was disbanded turned up post-war, in our house in Scotland. Not nearly so well conserved by us, but still the remnants of a saucer or cup will surface.

Loading a car with family luggage can be a challenge, and after loading the car for a trip to Scotland with, as we thought, commendable skill, we were sure that there was not a space left. Then Minnie appeared with a parcel insisting it must be added. When asked what it was and why it was so vital, she confessed it contained seven umbrella frames which she was sure would come in useful at some moment. After the war, when my Wren uniform became redundant, she appropriated it, and wore the hat to her dying day. Shoes were a hazard as she would take on any shoes she found and frequently they fitted badly. This resulted in her slipping and falling on Perth Station. When the paramedics picked her up, they pointed out the ill-fitting shoes to her. She addressed them sternly: 'In England we have non-skid pavements.' When she found herself with a room on a street, she would be delighted as she could then live by the light of the street lamp.

Animals were also important. She always managed to have a dog or cat, and in our nursery days she would nurture our guinea pigs, or dogs and above all she loved the canary which she would insist on taking to Austria with us every holidays, never being prepared to trust it to anyone else's care.

She lived well into her nineties and ended up in a bedsitter on the King's Road, where the constant flow of people going past her window delighted her. She had the requisite street light outside. When we gave her a coloured television we found she turned the colour off as she believed that saved electricity. She argued and cheered the programmes and particularly enjoyed Wimbledon and the tantrums of McEnroe and Năstase. But she was sure the majority of the programmes were pure moonshine or fantasy. She never believed in the moon landings, claiming they were typical stories of boys' healthy imaginations. 'Who'd want to drive round the moon? You'd run out of benzine.'

When I married, she electrified us all by giving us our dining room table and chairs, still in use. When Laura married, she got a cheque for £100 pounds, a large sum of money in 1952. Reggie said he was a bit relieved as he had always feared she had never been paid. She left Laura and me all her money.

My share went to buying the first tractor on my son Robert's fish farm.

LIFE MOVES ON –
OR THE STORY OF A HOUSE

Argyll is on the west coast of Scotland. For centuries it has been the home of the Clan Campbell, with Inveraray, the home of the Dukes of Argyll, the original county capital standing at its heart on Loch Fyne.

One of the ancient buildings in Argyll is Ardchattan Priory on the shores of Loch Etive. It was founded in the 12th century as a monastery of the Valliscaulian Order and it is thought it housed about 12 monks headed by a Prior. Before this the original settlement was made by a sixth century Saint, St Modan, an adherent of St Columba and the ruins of his original building is claimed to be on the hill where there is a well, known as St Modan's Well, where drink taken in a cup provided and accompanied by a small financial contribution will fulfil any wish.

Ardchattan is full of legends and ghost stories. It is said to be the second oldest house in Scotland still inhabited, as it has been since the 12th century. When the Reformation took over and the Priory was disbanded, the property was made over to a Lay Prior – a Campbell, and from then on the family who live there have always been descended from that Campbell.

Thus, in time, it became the home of the Campbell-Prestons.

During the war my mother-in-law and I lived there together for three years. Life didn't really change tremendously from pre-war ways until the war had been going for about a year. There was still a house full of domestics. Kate the Cook presided over the kitchen with its coal-fired range; Annie was parlourmaid and Mary housemaid. At that time the electricity was provided by a generator in the back yard. This gave us electric light, but there were no extras, such as electric kettles or electric irons or a Hoover, let alone central heating or electric fires. So the manual labour needed to keep the house even moderately warm was vital. Coal and wood, both heavy to handle, were lugged round the house to keep fires going in the sitting room and bedrooms.

In 1940 the Highland Division were captured in France. This cut a tremendous swathe through Scotland and one of the heavy losses was the Oban Battery, besides many men missing from Scotch regiments. A lot of problems arose immediately.

The question of pay had to be worked out and this took the War Office some time to get through. It meant great financial worry and need amongst the families. The financial difficulties meant that there were hard pressed families, especially among those whose breadwinners had volunteered as Territorials, and had enjoyed a better income in civilian life than Army pay. My mother-in-law in the Red Cross immediately began a depot to try and help with this problem.

When parcels were allowed to be sent to the prisoners in the form of clothes, this was often an added expense, so the depot expanded to help deal with this. My mother-in-law collected a group of volunteers, and took to touring quite far afield to be certain that everyone would know what help was available.

Amongst her contacts was Mrs Duncan McInnes, the wife of the Episcopalian vicar in the Church at Glencoe. Duncan himself was serving as a padre in the army and had therefore been captured with the rest of them. The McInneses were old friends as there had always been a practice to let Ardchattan in the summer holidays and often the family had decamped to a rented house in Glencoe.

Duncan's and my husband Patrick's paths crossed often as they moved about between German prison camps. Finally they both ended in Colditz where Duncan was an especially respected and valued member of the community.

After the war, when we came to live in Argyll, he was a friend we saw frequently and with pleasure. He was a tall, solid figure, liberal in his views and extremely good company, with always some good anecdote to tell. He talked with a deep voice, slowly, rolling his "Rs" and with deliberation. When Patrick was in hospital in Oban, two of his favourite visitors were Duncan and the Roman Catholic Bishop who had also been a prisoner with them.

One anecdote that Duncan used to tell was of a small boy who came back tired from school to have his mother put prunes and custard in front of him for his tea. He looked disgusted at this dish and said gloomily 'five bloody prunes again.' His mother, shocked at the rudeness of his language, sent him to his room telling him to ask God to forgive him. After the little boy had been in his room for a while, there was a tremendous thunderstorm. Knowing that her son was always scared in a thunderstorm, the mother thought she should relent and see how he was. She listened at the door and heard her small son saying: 'God, what a COMMOTION for FIVE bloody prunes!'

Duncan went on to become Bishop of Murray Ross and Caithness. At a service in Inverness Cathedral when he was preaching, Patrick, rather to my embarrassment, became restless during the sermon, glancing at his watch and shaking his head at the pulpit. After church when Duncan came to greet us, Patrick said 'Duncan how could you? It was a rotten sermon at the time and we told you never to do it again.' The text of the sermon had been: 'If asked to go half a mile go a mile.' Duncan had rather unfortunately preached this in a prison camp after a certain number of his congregation, who had managed to escape, had been recaptured. Suffering from blisters and sore feet after having 'gone a mile', the feeling was that on that occasion it might have been wiser to go only half a mile. Duncan rebutted Patrick by telling him that in future he wanted previous notice before Patrick came to hear him preach.

Duncan was a mighty prop and stay for me after Patrick died. He conducted Patrick's funeral service and subsequently the marriage of Alastair Campbell and Mary Ann, my elder daughter. He was always defusing problems which seemed to arise. If in need of a wise arbiter, Duncan was there. Mary Ann and Alastair's wedding was due to take place six weeks after Patrick died, which caused some soul-searching as to whether this was seemly. They consulted Duncan. He said: 'Alastair, you are a soldier, your father, and your father-in-law were soldiers, their fathers were soldiers, and a good soldier always goes forward and never looks back.'

Duncan's death a bit later was a considerable loss.

Through the centuries Ardchattan has received a number of alterations, each generation adapting it to their special need. My parents-in-law extended a nursery wing, but as the windows looked over an ancient cemetery attached to the Priory that was still in use, my mother-in-law succeeded in getting this closed. She felt it was not suitable for children to have funerals under their windows. It is renowned as the burial place for Colin Campbell of Glenure, the victim of the Appin Murder, the story of which inspired the book *Kidnapped* by Robert Louis Stevenson.

In the last generation, my sister-in-law, Angela, decided it was time the history of the Priory should be brought up to date and she appealed for help to Charles Fraser of Reelig in Invernesshire, who was a scholar of Scottish history and also a genealogist of some note. Ian was married to our eldest sister-in-law, Cherry, and held a somewhat senior position in the family. All his life he had bad health, losing a kidney in his teenage years, a desperate operation in those days. Dogged by this ill health, he never fulfilled his potential in life. At Oxford his friends and contemporaries included Roger Makins, who became distinguished in many spheres, amongst them as our Ambassador in Washington. Another friend was Evelyn Baring, who became Governor of Kenya and Zimbawe, and High Commissioner in South Africa.

Before the war, despite his poor health, Ian had become a territorial in the Lovat Scouts. He was also a benign landlord at Reelig, a member of Inverness County Council, and Albany Herald on account of his genealogical knowledge.

After the German invasion of Norway in the war, the Lovat Scouts were called up. They were sent to garrison the Faroe Islands. Before going to war Ian had given a power of attorney to his wife. The first thing she discovered was that her husband was giving a copy of *The Spectator* and *New Statesman* weekly, free, to every tenant on his estate. Shortly after arriving in the Faroe Islands, his wife Cherry noticed that cheques were being paid rather mysteriously to a nunnery on the islands. A number of officers in the Lovat Scouts were Roman Catholics and Ian had discovered that they were sending their laundry for the nuns to wash and, since no offer of payment had been made, typically Ian had paid himself. He was an unworldly man.

There was a story in the family that Ian had once held a considerable number of Fortnum and Mason shares. When there was a takeover bid for Fortnum's it was found that Ian held the controlling number of these shares. On discovering this, the putative buyer asked Ian to luncheon at the Ritz in London and explained that he badly needed these shares to win the deal. Ian of course could have held him to ransom for a substantial sum of money; instead, without any bargaining, he sold his share at the going price saying that the buyer was such a nice young man. Ian's stockbroker despaired. The family added the final part to this story by saying that the young man had been so surprised he had fainted and left the Ritz on a stretcher. This is probably an apocryphal story but for all that it was perfectly possible.

Ian could have become a successful writer. During the war and later when he went to Italy to work in Intelligence, he used to write letters totally divorced from the subject of the war, and they were usually perfect small essays.

In *The Country Gentlemen's Magazine* there would appear advertisements for second-hand sales. There was one for a long black velvet evening dress which the advertiser said had only been worn once. Ian wrote me a letter based on this and investigated imagined reasons for such a swift sale of a clearly valued possession. He speculated that it had perhaps been worn by the subject at a dinner party and, being no doubt considerably décolleté, the lady had had a flirtatious evening to the fury of her husband who had insisted that she sold the dress at once.

Also during the war it could be difficult to get the newspapers on time and there were advertisements in papers with people offering to sell on their old newspapers on a weekly basis, so that one could be reading a daily newspaper a week or so late. Ian wrote another letter describing how the news could be read with equal pleasure ten days later. One of the sadnesses of my life is that I never succeeded in keeping these letters for posterity because they were remarkable, written as they were from a war zone.

So it was typical that he did a considerable job of research before writing in his masterly prose the history of Ardchattan up to date.

But Ian had an irrepressible sense of humour and could not resist writing a second document which was a spoof of the more serious one. He told my brother-in-law Bobby, whom he maintained he had discovered is entitled to be the hereditary Prior, that he regretted to say that the Prior of Ardchattan's powers of punishment would appear to be only spiritual and he added: 'I can find no authority for the physical application.' He added, and emphasised that this was true, not a spoof, that though he could not find this in the rules of the Order 'you may like to know that paper was rare and expensive in the Middle Ages and that old monastic gowns were the normal substitute for Bronco and Bromo (two well-known brands of lavatory paper in our day); the remnants of such have been (literally) unearthed in Medieval Monastic Privies. The Valliscaulians were Burgundians, that is to say 'continentals.' This explained why they were provided with underclothes only when travelling ....'

There were two legends belonging to the house that seemed possible to verify. One room in the medieval building, always known as the Prior's Room, had an Oratory leading from it. The story went that one Prior became enamoured of a nun who lived in a nunnery over the loch. She came to visit him one day, and during her visit, the Prior of Ardchattan's Superior, the Prior of Beauly, inconveniently turned up. The Prior quickly hid her in the Oratory, but the visitor stayed so long that the poor nun died and was buried under the floor. During some repairs to the Oratory, Archie Campbell the builder found some bones. These he collected reverently in a shoebox, and with his hat removed delivered them to Bobby, who equally reverentially handed them to the doctor for analysis. Shortly the doctor broke the news that it was a fine collection of rabbit bones.

Another tale was of Bishop Carswell, Bishop of Argyll and the Isles. Ian set out to research this as Bishop Carswell was an eminent churchman who had translated John Knox's liturgy into the Gaelic. There was a notion that he was buried under the floor of what had been the monk's Refectory. Ian discovered that it was originally part 'undercroft' and part 'calefactory' but was currently the Ping Pong room.

Ian wrote to report: 'Just when I'd hoped the Right Rev Duncan McInnes would have confirmed (or otherwise) that Bishop John Carswell's Gaelic translation of John Knox's liturgy was or was not, still in use by the Episcopalian Church in Scotland, I've had a charming letter back saying in effect he does not know! However, he does tell me to consult one Presbyterian Minister and one Roman Catholic Divine and to mention his name as introduction, which just shows what a liberal minded man he is.' Ian did discover that Bishop Carswell was described as 'of powerful physique', and that he was 'a grasping man of enormous size.' So he advises against any effort to disinter him. As Ian said: 'Ping Pong was unknown to him, by all accounts, and he would easily have been champion if he chose to rise up and join the game.'

The true facts about him are known. Carswell built the Castle of Carnasserie near Kilmartin. When he died his body was brought through the hills to be buried at Ardchattan. As they crossed Loch Etive the towrope parted and the barge they were towing, on which rested the coffin, vanished in the murk.

The next day the loch was mirror calm and the coffin was found a couple of hundred yards from the Priory, washed ashore on what is known to this day as 'Carswell's Point.'

After the cemetery was closed, (it had adjoined the ruined Chapel, by some claimed to have been burnt down by Cromwell's troops, by others as having simply fallen down after neglect), the Ministry of Works started excavations, wanting to map definitively the location of the Cloisters etc. One day the workman digging out the foundation of the Chapel found a body, a skeleton almost seven feet tall. This was almost certainly Carswell. Whenever the assumption that Carswell was buried in the Chapel was mentioned to my brother-in-law, Bobby, he became almost incandescent. 'Nonsense, I know exactly where he is, he's under the scullery sink.'

So there stands Ardchattan, and it's nice to know that there exist all over the country, so many ancient monuments that have survived the centuries, where progress and history intermingle. Now, where the monks once ate (according to their irreverent chronicler, as their Order, translated, means the Order of the Cabbage) a diet of cabbages, today, in their Refectory computers twinkle, and news can be accessed from all over the world almost instantaneously. I doubt if they would have enjoyed that. But probably they would have enjoyed some Marks and Spencer underclothes.

I think it can be pointed out that life does move on.

EPILOGUE

So where have 80 or 90 years got us? As we wise old heads nod together, we say the world has certainly changed. Materially it has certainly changed, but I don't believe human nature has changed very much.

Personally I seem to have come a long way in life from the little girl, living in houses where there was only one telephone. The whole world of communication was so totally different.

My generation has lived through a revolution as far as communications and scientific advancement are concerned. I have to admit that I am now engaged in a love/irritation relationship with the computer. It is time-consuming and fascinating. Quite often it is extremely irritating, but that is the challenge. This short book was written on a computer which has a marvellous facility by which you talk to your computer and it does the typing, usually with accuracy, but occasionally an entertaining mistake. It is as well to explain to anyone who may be listening that you are not addressing long conversations to yourself.

At my elbow is my cordless telephone and besides that my filofax with a list of mobile telephone numbers of my friends and relations. I can and frequently do not have the faintest idea where I may be ringing them. For all I know, they may be in their baths, riding a camel in the Arabian desert, weeding the garden or having an intimate conversation with their doctor, not to mention driving along a motorway, or lurking in a lay-by outside Glasgow.

Equally on my computer I have a programme called Skype, which enables me to ring up my daughter in Scotland and talk to her face to face as if she was in the same room. I can do the same to my granddaughter in Bermuda or my nephew in New Zealand. Skyping a great-granddaughter, she wanted me to meet her hamster and I found myself eyeball to eyeball with a very surprised hamster. The surprise was quite mutual.

Then there is e-mail, a poor substitute for a proper letter as one has doubts about its safety from being read by anybody. For rapidity of contact and all basic news it is superior to the telegram if inferior to the letter. There are considerable elements in this new instrument which are frightening to some of us oldies. The thought of programmes called Facebook, blogs and Twitter are not very encouraging.

One of the interesting experiences of old age is to find that one is History and to view programmes on the television covering the events one has lived through. Often the commentaries strike one as quite odd and not at all in line with one's own memory. But there are many good things to remember in the course of a long life. Perhaps it is a good moment to start and finish with the fact that when I was three years old, women got the vote.